The Poetry of Events

The Poetry of Events

Daniel Webster's Rhetoric of the Constitution and Union

Paul D. Erickson

NEW YORK UNIVERSITY PRESS
New York & London

Library of Congress Cataloging-in-Publication Data

Erickson, Paul D., 1954–
  The poetry of events.

  Bibliography: p.
  Includes index.
  1. Webster, Daniel, 1782–1852—Oratory. 2. Webster,
Daniel, 1782–1852—Language. 3. Political oratory—
United States. 4. United States—Politics and
government—1815–1861. I. Title.
E340.W4E75   1986   973.5'092'4   86–18104
ISBN 0–8147–2170–2

Book Design by Ken Venezio

*This work is dedicated to Jack Ziegler,
my first and finest teacher.*

But in regard to this country, there is no poetry like the poetry of events; and the prophecies lag behind their fulfillment.

Daniel Webster
November 7, 1849

Contents

Introduction

In July of 1853, Rufus Choate stood before the students, faculty, and alumni of Dartmouth College and spoke of his old friend, Daniel Webster. A protégé and colleague, Choate reviewed Webster's life and work, commented on his accomplishments, and lamented his passing. Trying to explain the essence of Webster's life and the source of his power both political and personal, Choate said, "Such eminence and such hold on the public mind as he attained demands extraordinary general intellectual power, adequate mental culture, an impressive, attractive, energetic, and great character, and extraordinary specific power also of influencing the convictions of others by speech."[1]

Every student of Webster recognizes that his skill with language played a central part in his work, yet few have tried with much effort to understand his rhetoric per se. Such analysis has dangers. We could find ourselves caught up in Webster's flourishes and purple passages, responding more to the splendors of his words than to the ideas and thought behind them. And style is an elusive quality, the examination of which can often be murderous, leaving only a dissected cadaver with no hint of its former life and charm. It can be mystifying; as Choate said of listening to Webster,

"[A]lthough it left you a very good witness of his power of influencing others, you were not in the best condition immediately to pronounce on the quality or the source of the influence. You saw the flash and heard the peal, and felt the admiration and fear; but from what region it was launched, and by what divinity, and from what Olympian seat, you could not certainly yet tell."[2]

To understand Webster, Choate suggested that we "look through the crystal water of the style down to the golden sands of the thought."[3] This advice has been the cardinal rule of the best historical and legal studies of Webster and his career. But at the same time it has caused scholars to look less carefully at Webster's language. By assuming that his speeches are only "crystal water," that style should be avoided as it if were a dangerous seduction and not a matter of real import, we miss an essential part of Webster's power. His ideas, his understanding of American history, and the ways in which he used tough lawyerly analysis and logic to construe the laws of this country are the core of Webster's work, but without his genius as a man of letters, I think that he would have accomplished a good deal less than he did.

The subject of this extended essay is the flash and the peal of Webster's words as manifested in his speeches on behalf of the Constitution and Union. Rather than analyze the development of Webster's constitutionalism, as others have done very well, I concentrate on "the crystal water," aiming to show that it is not transparent at all, but that Webster's style is quite often actually his substance, at least in its most important effects on the American people. Webster was beyond any doubt an artist. He presented two visions of America: prosaic legal discourses constituted the bulk of his speeches, but their greatest effect came from the poetic imagery, dramatic passages, quasi-fictitious characters, mythic histories, and apocalyptic prophecies. Emerson believed Webster one of the most eloquent men of his age, comparing him to Shakespeare and pronouncing his speeches the poetic embodiments of America. In a sense, Webster was one of America's most important poets, and it makes some sense to suggest that Webster's literary creations moved the nation toward the Civil War.

Webster scholarship is less than abundant. While a good deal has been written and pronounced about him, suprisingly little of it is useful. A number of bad panegyrical biographies exist, making the legend of Dan'l Webster something of a mainstay in the popular imagination. Several very good studies of Webster are available, however. George Ticknor Curtis' massive *Life of Daniel Webster* is rich in detail and insight, even though biased by its author's devotion to Webster.[4] Claude Fuess' *Daniel Webster* offers less information, but it is pleasantly written.[5] Richard Current's *Daniel Webster and the Rise of National Conservatism* employs more modern scholarly methods but is disappointingly short.[6] By far the best biographies of Webster are Irving Bartlett's *Daniel Webster* and Maurice Baxter's *One and Inseparable: Daniel Webster and the Union.*[7] These exceptionally thoughtful and useful books combine attention to detail with critical acumen. Any consideration of Webster and his work should begin with Bartlett and Baxter.

Baxter's *Daniel Webster and the Supreme Court* treats thoroughly Webster's work as an attorney and analyzes the legal counterpart to the poetic vision of the Union that I undertake.[8] Norman D. Brown's *Daniel Webster and the Politics of National Availability* considers Webster's partisan activities between

1828 and 1835 specifically in regard to the attempt to parlay his new fame as the Slayer of Nullification into a serious presidential nomination.[9] Sydney Nathans' *Daniel Webster and Jacksonian Democracy* covers the same subject, extending its scope to 1844.[10] Robert Dalzell's *Daniel Webster and the Trial of American Nationalism* follows Webster from 1843 to his death in 1852. Professor Dalzell argues persuasively that Webster recognized the sometimes political marketability of Unionism, but that he also knew that supporting the Compromise of 1850 could ruin him.[11]

All of the above writers acknowledge Webster's oratorical brilliance, but few of them analyze it. Biographers usually quote, paraphrase, and applaud the famous speeches; historians find Webster's theses more interesting than his technique. Six studies on Webster's language do deserve special mention, though. Edwin Percy Whipple's "Daniel Webster as a Master of English Style" is more appreciation than criticism, but Whipple offers some good insights into how Webster developed and into how he differed from his contemporaries.[12] Wilbur Samuel Howell and Hoyt Hopewell Hudson wrote a superb essay on Webster in Brigance's *A History and Criticism of American Public Address*.[13] Along with carefully studying Webster's stylistic strategies, Howell and Hudson show how Webster manipulated audiences by balancing fact and fiction, statistics and poetry. Paul C. Nagel, throughout *One Nation Indivisible: The Union in American Thought: 1776–1861* and *This Sacred Trust: American Nationality, 1798–1898*, reveals much about how Webster and others created and used poetic language to capture their vision of the United States.[14] Ferenc M. Szasz, in a short essay entitled "Daniel Webster—Architect of America's Civil Religion," sees Webster's speeches as proof that Webster believed that God had singled out America for a divine purpose.[15] Robert A. Ferguson, writing in his *Law and Letters in American Culture*, gives the best account of how Webster's legal training affected his discourse.[16] Ferguson's is an excellent analysis, one that I hope my own work on Webster's poetic instincts will complement.

I would like to thank several people for their part in this enterprise. First, George Jepsen, who helped me figure out what I was doing in my first explorations of Webster. Kevin Van Anglen shared his wisdom and insights, as did John Hildebidle. Tim Bent gave me ideas and kept me company, and Chenoweth Moffatt made the whole experience immensely more fun than it would have been without her. I also thank William H. Fowler of *The New England Quarterly* for his editorial advice on a portion of this work, and Kitty Moore, Despina Gimbel, Colin Jones, and Robin Berson. Special thanks go to Little, Brown and Company for giving me permission to quote from their fine 1903 National Edition of *The Writings and Speeches of Daniel Webster* edited by James McIntyre. A National Endowment for the Humanities Constitutional Fellowship for Independent Study and Research and the hospitality of Harvard's Charles Warren Center and —as always—of Quincy House made the entire project possible. Thank you all.

The Poetry of Events

1. The Defender of the Union

Daniel Webster's political career ended in anger and humiliation on June 21, 1852, when the Whig National Convention nominated Winfield Scott for the presidency. Arrangements between incumbent President Millard Fillmore and Secretary of State Webster collapsed at the Baltimore convention, and Southern delegates withheld adequate support for the man who had sacrificed Northern votes by coming out for the Fugitive Slave Law. After fifty-three ballots, Webster ran third: Scott's votes outnumbered his by seven to one. For decades, Webster had wanted the Presidency and more than once had thought it within reach, but in 1852 his last effort brought only embarrassing defeat.

To comfort their friend, the Webster Committee of Correspondence met quickly back in Boston and decided to give him a splended reception on his return home. In a grand and more than slightly ironic gesture, Boston welcomed Webster as a triumphant hero on the afternoon of July 9. A procession met him at the Boston-Roxbury line and escorted him into the center of town. Shopkeepers closed their doors early, citizens displayed portraits and busts of Webster along his route, and mothers held their children aloft "that they might say, in after life, they had seen the Defender of the Constitution on his triumphal entry into Boston."[1] An immense audience gathered on the Common to hear J. Thomas Stevenson welcome Webster and thank him for his services to the state and nation. Proclaiming Webster "THE AMERICAN," Stevenson thanked him "for what you have done to enshrine the Constitution of our country upon the inner altar of the temple of our hearts. We greet you as its greatest defender: . . . We greet you as the Champion of the Union." (vol. 13, p. 531).

Many Bostonians did love and honor Webster, but the event was nonetheless something of a sham. Since March 7, 1850, his reputation had fallen. As a voice of compromise defending the Fugitive Slave Law, he stood at odds with the radical abolitionism growing ever stronger in Boston. Webster was an outcast in 1852, blasted as an opportunistic traitor to his earlier antislavery convictions—no matter how grand a show of support his friends could orchestrate. Stevenson's panegyric notwithstanding, Webster himself had few illusions about his circumstances, and the speech that he delivered on the occasion hardly expesses the joyful benediction of an aging hero to his beloved followers. On the contrary, beneath a thin veneer of politeness the speech was a bitter self-defense and an angry attack on his political enemies. Two weeks later Webster would give a farewell address to his neighbors in Marshfield, warmly recalling "not an unkind thing done, nor word spoken to me or mine."[2] The Boston speech contrasts quite sharply. After reminding his audience of Boston's original loyalty to "the whole of America, as a country," Webster spoke ruefully about his relationship to Massachusetts.[3] In 1823, the year of his first election to Congress as a Representative from Boston, the state had been entirely loyal to the Union, he said, allowing him to serve it happily and with pride. Webster said many kind things about Massachusetts—but he put all of his praise in the past tense: "That was the Massachusetts which I had honored, historically, from the Revolution downwards," he lamented; "History tells us what Massachusetts was, when she did me the honor to call me into her service. . . ." (vol. 13, p. 537). Webster did not criticize Massachusetts outright in 1852, but neither did he have much complimentary to say about its present generation. This omission and his angry nostalgia suggest that Webster felt forced to choose between his adopted state and his vision of the American Union, and that he chose the latter.

Webster's sense of the nation had lost much currency by 1852 in Boston. Many there found union with slave states anathema. As early as 1829, William Lloyd Garrison had spoken of "the guilt and danger of destroying the bodies and souls of men *as the price of saving our Union.*"[4] In 1844 he wrote, "The Union which grinds [the slaves] to dust rests upon us and with them we will struggle to overthrow it!"[5] And in 1850, Wendell Phillips reviewed Webster's "Constitution and Union" speech, proclaiming, "we would be rid of this Union, because experience has shown it to be, in its character and construction, an insurmountable obstacle to the *HARMONY* of the nation."[6] (Of course, the resistance to the Compromise Measures was far from universal in the early 1850s, but Webster saw the movement as ominous and felt the barbs of his critics with sensitivity perhaps made more acute by personal tradition and political ambition.)

Phillips' distinction between unity and harmony depends on the assumption that the American nation and its government were not identical, and that the administrative structures of the country established by the Constitution were neither fixed nor even essential. The view that "America" could exist in some sense independent of its Constitution runs throughout antebellum history. Colonial leaders did not originally see their thirteen countries as one; alliances and the Confederation arose to solve particular problems, with the notion of national unity evolving slowly and never with total success. As temporary arrangements proved unable to meet the needs of the newly independent states, the old Articles of Confederation gave way to the Constitution. Ratification and adoption did not end Anti-Federalism, though. A strong doctrine of states' rights persisted up to (and to a reduced extent after) the surrender at Appomattox. Wendell Philips' argument had counterparts in the Essex Junto, the Hartford Convention, the South Carolina Proclamation, and the Confederate States of America. For all their determination, however, the descendants of the Anti-Federalists lost to adherents of "one nation indivisible." Over the decades, many Americans came to consider their Union as more than an effective administrative solution to their common problems. With time and the rise of a new generation (to which Daniel Webster belonged), the Union became in the eyes of most people an object worthy of devotion in and of itself. For Unionists, preservation of the government became a tenet of civil religion. When Abraham Lincoln called the Union "perpetual" in his first inaugural address, he chose an adjective with mystical as well as legal connotations.[7]

Daniel Webster did more than any other single individual in his lifetime to promote this concept of the perpetual Union. A Federalist by inheritance—his father reportedly refused to serve dissenters in his New Hampshire tavern—Webster first gained titles such as Defender of the Constitution in his 1830 debate with Robert Y. Hayne over nullification. Gaining national prominence from his eloquence on behalf of the Union in that quarrel, Webster identified himself more and more closely with nationalism in years to come. He presented nearly every important issue in terms of the Union, turning even fairly insignificant questions into tests of the nation's integrity. A favorite trope recalled Washington's "Farewell Address" reference to the Constitution as America's palladium, the locus of all the country's hopes and glories, without which the nation would fall like pillaged Troy. Fights over tariffs, slavery, and other policies convinced some Americans to give up on the Union. Even Webster went through a period during the War of 1812 when he entertained thoughts of secession. But by 1852 he had defended his Union so often and so determinedly that he could not be shaken.

Webster's critics thought his position outmoded and doomed; even in retrospect it might appear that since his and Henry Clay's Compromise of 1850 failed to preserve the Union without bloodshed, Webster took his stand in vain. Theodore Parker reviled Webster in a funeral discourse, declaring: "His influence on the development of America has not been great. He had large gifts, large opportunities also for their use, . . . yet he has brought little to pass. No great ideas, no great organizations, will bind him to the coming age."[8] Parker could not have been more wrong. Webster died a defeated man, but his vision of the Union survived and triumphed. In the midst of the war, Lincoln vindicated Webster when he wrote to Horace Greeley that his "paramount object in this struggle is to save the Union, and is not to save or destroy slavery."[9] Edwin Percy Whipple wrote, "When the great Civil War broke out, hundreds of thousands of American citizens marched to the battle-field with the grand passages of Webster glowing in their hearts."[10] Webster feared that the breakup of the Union would mean a mutually and totally destructive war. The irony of Webster's work to prevent war is that his celebration of the Union as an absolute necessity helped to bring it about. Further, the very war that he sought to avoid preserved his beloved nation intact in the end.

For all the fraudulence of the 1852 reception on the Boston Common, Stevenson nevertheless spoke accurately when he gave Webster credit for enshrining the Constitution in America's heart. A man of major accomplishments in legal, diplomatic and legislative matters, Webster did his most important work by preaching Unionism throughout the country. And the foundation of this achievement was his power with language. Lacking family connections, military renown, and political "availability," Webster gained his might from intelligence, hard work, and above all from his oratory. Legal and historical study gave Webster the facts and theories that he needed to support his positions; but eloquence gave his arguments life.

In his over fifty years of public speaking, Daniel Webster addressed crowds, legislative assemblies, and jurists on dozens of subjects, but no single topic played as prominent a part in Webster's speeches as did the constitutional Union— a fact highlighted by the title of Maurice Baxter's recent biography, *One and Inseparable: Daniel Webster and The Union.*[11] Webster's work on the Union was especially visible (and audible), but his concern was far from unique. In all the mass of speeches, pamphlets, sermons, and histories from the years between the Revolutionary and Civil Wars, the most common theme is easily the sense of novelty with which America viewed itself. This perception raised two apparently contradictory and equally important questions: Would the country survive? and What forms should it take in order to balance "liberty and union"? Speaking on Independence Day in 1806 to an audience in Concord, New Hampshire, Webster said that America

is the last of a little family of republics. She hath survived all her friends, and now exists, in the midst of an envious world, without the society of one nation with which she is associated by similarity of government and character. Whether it be possible to preserve this republican unit in existence and health, is the great question which perpetually fastens on the mind.[12]

The same uniqueness that isolated and frightened America also brought power and responsibility. "America is not now a small, remote star glimmering on the political concerns of Europe with a faint and cold beam," continued Webster; "She is in the new firmament, shining with a brilliance which cannot be disregarded." (vol. 15, p. 539). Even if Americans wished to escape the eyes of the world, they could not: blazing in the political heavens, the Union's light could not be dimmed. The question was whether that light would be the flash of a meteor or the steady light of a sun. And to that overarching question, Webster devoted more words than he did to any other. As he said in Concord, all questions were "important to the last degree, so far, and so far only, as they affect the integrity of the Constitution." (vol. 15, p. 537).

Just how much Webster himself valued his talent for oratory is illustrated by a passage from an 1851 speech in Buffalo in defense of the Fugitive Slave Law. Webster faced a formidable task: anger over the law was at a high pitch in the north, and upstate New York was an especially strong abolitionist center. Defending the constitutionality of the law and asserting that his listeners had a duty to obey it, Webster used a range of powerful legal and emotional arguments to make his case. Realizing the enormity of his task, and no doubt feeling a bit desperate in light of how much resistance the law encountered, Webster interrupted his speech with a remark that revealed his state of mind and also the way in which he perceived his role in the nation's destiny. "Gentlemen," he said, "I wish I had ten thousand voices. I wish I could draw around me the whole people of the United States, and I wish I could make them all hear what I now declare."[13]

The urgency of Webster's words shows how important he considered his talents as a man speaking, a confidence bred of decades before crowds that he had moved with his words. Language was the key to the major successes in Webster's life, the foundation of his legal, legislative, and diplomatic career. His knowledge of the law and of history was considerable, but more knowledgeable men than he, lacking his genius for communication, had had less effect on the nation. Considered a master of oratory in an age distinguished by brilliant rhetoric, Webster rose to great heights and profoundly influenced the course of American history by virtue of his way with words.

Webster's affinity for language began in his childhood. Recalling his early years in a short autobiographical essay, Webster remembered with special fondness—and emphasis— his youthful love of reading. "I do not remember when or by whom I was taught to read," he wrote, "because I cannot and never could recollect a time when I could not read the Bible." Supposing that either his mother or one of his elder sisters had taught him, Webster observed that like the rest of his family, his father "seemed to have no higher object in the world, than to educate his children."[14] Thanks in part to his father's efforts, a small circulating library serviced Webster's community. Webster proved a voracious reader, charging through volumes of the *Spectator* and anything else he could find. "I was fond of poetry," he wrote;

I remember that my father brought home from some of the lower towns Pope's Essay on Man, published in some sort of pamphlet. I took it, and very soon could repeat it, from beginning to end. We had so few books that to read them once or twice was nothing. We thought they were all to be got by heart.[15]

Even as a child, Webster associated literature with speaking aloud. Guests at his father's tavern often called on him to declaim a bit of verse or to read from the Bible, an experience that gave him a stock of ready quotations and allusions for decades to come, and that taught Webster about cadence and delivery, and of turning words and tropes into emotionally active—and by extension utilitarian—things.

The benefits of fireside reading and itinerant schoolmasters aside, Webster's father wanted more education for his son. Ebenezer Webster was a man of import in his day. A soldier in Washington's army (he stood guard outside the general's tent during the Benedict Arnold crisis), he served as a New Hampshire Elector and as a Representative to the state legislature. But he felt that a lack of formal education had held him back and urged his son, "Exert yourself, improve your opportunities, learn, learn."[16] To further this end, in 1796 the elder Webster decided to enroll his son in the school founded by John Phillips at Exeter, a relatively new academy opened a year before Webster was born. At home in Salisbury young Webster had a high reputation for his learning and wit; he was admired by the townsfolk and praised by his father's guests. At Exeter, though, Webster found himself in a much bigger pond. "I had never been away from home," he wrote later of his first days in the new school, "and the change overpowered me. I hardly remained master of my own senses, among ninety boys who had seen so much and appeared to know so much more than I did."[17] No longer the village prodigy, Webster felt awkward and intellectually ungainly—a hick, to put the matter succinctly.

Webster grew a bit more comfortable in the ensuing weeks, and did quite well in his classes, notably in English and

Classics. Curiously, though, he could not overcome his shyness and outright terror when it came to what had already been and what would later be his forte: public speaking. He recalled of this time:

> I believe I made tolerable progress in most branches which I attended to, but there was one thing I could not do. I could not make a declamation. I could not speak before the school. The kind and excellent Buckminster [Joseph Stevens Buckminster, a younger classmate who worked closely with Webster] sought especially, to persuade me to perform the exercise of declamation, like other boys; but I could not do it. Many a piece did I commit to memory, and recite and rehearse, in my own room, over and over again; yet when the day came, when the school collected to hear my declamations, when my name was called, and I saw all eyes turned to my seat, I could not raise myself from it. Sometimes the instructors frowned, sometimes they smiled. Mr. Buckminster always pressed and entreated, most winningly, that I would venture; but I could never command sufficient resolution. When the occasion was over I went home and wept bitter tears of mortification.[18]

Biographers have offered various explanations of Webster's terror. Most dismiss it as a simple case of stage fright on the part of a young boy surrounded by strangers. (Irving Bartlett suggests a deeper psychological explanation involving Webster's conflicting desires to please his father with success and yet to avoid surpassing the man.)[19] Whatever the cause, Webster spent too little time at Exeter to overcome its intimidations. His father brought Webster back to Salisbury after only a few months and found him a teaching job in the village's one-room school, where many of his students were older than he.

Webster might well have spent his life as a schoolteacher if not for the intervention of Samuel Wood, a minister from the neighboring town of Boscawen. Wood had met and been impressed by the young Webster, and iterated the father's advice to "learn"—in fact, he admonished Ebenezer for interrupting his son's schooling and urged him to let the boy prepare for college under his own tutelage. The proposal accepted, Ebenezer drove Daniel the six miles to Woods' home, announcing the scheme to the boy en route. Recalling the revelation in his autobiography, Webster described the joy and gratitude he felt realizing that his father would support his education: "The very idea thrilled my whole frame . . . A warm glow ran all over me, and I laid my head on my father's shoulder, and wept."[20]

Wood, who had himself graduated from Dartmouth, had good qualifications to act as Webster's tutor. He had tutored over a hundred students for entry into college, and had a fairly regular course in classics designed for his charge. Webster stayed with Wood for only seven months, but that short time proved valuable and delightful. Wood and David Palmer, a Dartmouth senior visiting the Reverend, took Webster through Greek and Latin and generally guided his reading and thinking. Along with his formal study, Webster read as widely as he could, taking advantage of the Boscawen Social Library, whose two hundred books far surpassed the small library available to him at Salisbury. He took particular joy in *Don Quixote:* "I began to read it, and it is literally true that I never closed my eyes till I had finished it; nor did I lay it down for five minutes, so great was the power of that extraordinary book upon my imagination."[21] These months spent away from home yet still in a homely environment combining family life with study seem to have suited Webster perfectly and made his eventual transition to Dartmouth much smoother than his arrival at Exeter had been. In the early fall of 1796, Webster left Boscawen and after stopping in Salisbury to tie a feather bed to his horse and gather what few belongings he had, Daniel rode off to Hanover, New Hampshire.

Founded in 1769 by Eleazar Wheelock—Webster's father chaired the legislative committee that awarded the land for the school—ostensibly as an Indian college, Dartmouth was in Webster's day already one of the leading and largest colleges in the United States. The graduating classes between 1796 and 1800 averaged thirty-six students, second only to Harvard's at that time. Ruled by John Wheelock, Eleazar's son, the school had four professors and three younger tutors who had themselves but recently graduated from the college. Most activities took place in Dartmouth Hall, a large central building that had a small dormitory, some classrooms, and a small library.

The library was the work of Eleazar Wheelock, who put great store on books and their availability for students. Although putatively the pride of Hanover, this collection was in truth rather lamentable. Given Wheelock's evangelistic nature (which was quite appropriate at a time when colleges existed largely to train clergy), the library contained books primarily on religion, many of them donated to his enterprise by pious friends and supporters. Under the supervision of John Smith—a peculiar man who taught languages and literature despite a characteristic nervousness that frequently left him helpless in class, and to whom students referred as "Professor Johnny"[22]—the collection increased to upwards of three thousand volumes by Webster's graduation. Expand though it did in bulk, however, Dartmouth's official library stayed slight in variety and scope. Religious wisdom and sentiment remained the dominant topics, and many of the books were duplicates. Even if they had been of interest, students had little access to them; after paying an annual user's fee of a dollar and a half, they could take advantage of the library's one open hour every two weeks—provided that no more than five students sought entrance at once. And they could use books only after the librarian took them down from the shelves. Borrowing privileges were commensurate: freshman could take out one book, sophomores and juniors two, and seniors three.[23]

The academic policies under which Webster studied had been set by the "Laws to be observed by members of Dartmouth College" enacted by the trustees in 1796, the year before Webster arrived. Admission required evidence of "good moral character" and a day of oral examinations to guarantee that candidates "be versed in Virgil, Cicero's Select Orations, the Greek Testament, be able accurately to translate English into Latin and also understand the fundimental [sic] rules of arithmetic."[24] Like other students, Webster spent his first day in Hanover marching dutifully between the homes of faculty examiners and finally reporting to the president's house for word of his admission. Having succeeded in this campaign of application, he began four years of studying the curriculum set out by the 1796 Laws:

> It shall be the duty of the student to study the languages, sciences at the college in the following order, viz: The Freshmen, the Latin and Greek classics, Arithmetic, English Grammar, Rhetoric & the Elements of Criticism.—The Sophimores [sic] Latin, and Greek classics, Logic, Arithmetic, Geography, Geometry, Trigonometry, Algebra, Conic Sections, Surveying, mensuration of heights and distances & the Belle Lettres.—The Juniors the Latin and Greek Classics, Geometry, Natural and Moral Philosophy, Astronomy.—The Seniors Metaphysics, Theology & Natural and Politic Law.—The study of Hebrew and other oriental languages as also of the French language is recommended to the students.—All the classes shall attend to composition and speaking as the authority may direct. Members of the classes in rotation shall declaim before the officers in the chapel on every Wednesday at two o'clock in the afternoon. And on the first Wednesday in every month the members of the Senior class shall hold forensic disputations in the chapel immediately after declamations. At the exercises all students are required to be present.[25]

Two things in particular stand out in this list: the emphasis that the Trustees put on practical education in subjects such as surveying, and the paramount attention that they paid to teaching students how to use the English language to com-

13

municate—especially in public speaking. This pervasive training in rhetoric fit right into the overall utilitarian scheme: of the 234 men who graduated in classes with which Webster had contact, 41 percent became lawyers; 25 percent ministers; and 12 percent teachers. More than three-quarters, in other words, chose careers that required rhetorical skills.[26]

Formal schooling at Dartmouth was good, but as is often the case for the best college students, Webster's better and by far more important education came from his extracurricular enterprises. Much of what the intellectually straight-laced faculty could not teach, Webster and his classmates taught themselves, and they did so by way of fraternities. The most important of these were the two literary societies, the Social Friends and the United Fraternity, both founded in the 1780s. Nearly every student belonged to one of these two clubs, and competition for prominent members was keen—sometimes so keen, in fact, that the administration eventually simply assigned incoming students to the rival organizations arbitrarily. The literary societies performed two vital functions that added immeasurably to the value of four years spent at Hanover. First, they held exercises in public speaking that far surpassed those ordained by the college. Debates, prepared orations, and commencement dialogues all gave opportunities for the future lawyers, ministers, and teachers to practice thinking and talking on their feet. And the societies made up for Professor Johnny's dubious library by building splendid collections for use by members.

Daniel Webster joined the United Fraternity and served that year as its "Inspector of Books." He advanced through the ranks, becoming in turn Librarian, Orator, Vice President, and as a senior, President. Gone were the days of his awkward timidity at Exeter; at Dartmouth, Webster gained the admiration of all for his rhetorical genius. "We used to listen to him," wrote one classmate, "with the deepest interest and respect, and no one thought of equalling the vigor and glow of his eloquence."[27] Easily the best speaker on campus, Webster had the rare honor of being asked, despite his youth, to deliver the July Fourth address for Hanover in 1800. Although not a fair indication of what Webster would one day accomplish, the talk did please its listeners immensely, and appeared soon afterwards in pamphlet form. The school also called on Webster to present a eulogy for a student who died in 1801. That same summer, Webster's oratorical reputation precipitated an uncomfortable episode involving the commencement address. The usual practice decreed that the students themselves would choose their valedictory and salutatory speakers, but that year the students could not agree and the faculty made the choice—and they did not choose Daniel Webster. With the full support of the United Fraternity, Webster refused to take part in the program (in which he had been offered an "inferior" position as orator on an assigned topic), although he did deliver a speech to the fraternity on the subject of received opinion and independent thinking. This episode and Webster's possible part in it (one college rumor held that he tore up his diploma in fury) have been the stuff of a greater debate among biographers than they could possibly deserve to be. The important point to the story is that it shows how highly the student community esteemed Webster as a speaker and as a leader. As he would for the rest of his life, Webster had won power and authority with words.

After graduation, Webster began to study law back in Salisbury, but his own and his family's financial straits forced him to take up his old work of teaching school. He taught in Fryeburg, Maine for a few months, enjoying his young bachelor's life of reading, writing odd bits of verse and essays, corresponding with friends, and generally playing the dashing young man about town. The charms of this life wore thin, though, and despite being offered a raise by the school, Webster left in the autumn to resume his preparation for the bar as an apprentice to Thomas Thompson, a Salisbury attorney and future congressman.

Although he had chosen this career, Webster found reading law far less engaging than his literary pursuits. He wrote to a friend, "This law reading, Thomas, has no tendency to add to the embellishments of literature to a student's acquisitions. Our books are written in a hard, didactic style, interspersed on every page with the mangled pieces of murdered Latin, and as perfectly barren of all elegance as a girl's cheek is of a beard."[28] Nonetheless, Webster persisted; he moved to Boston to start a new apprenticeship in the offices of Christopher Gore, a pominent attorney and diplomat who had just returned from an extended mission to England for the government. As he had at Dartmouth, Webster made the most of his surroundings. Studying with great but not excessive industry, he made important new friendships among the city's gentry, and he traveled throughout the region. By 1805 Webster was ready to move on. Although city life attracted him powerfully, he felt out of filial duty that he should move back within easy reach of his aging parents. His father helped win him an appointment as Clerk of Common Pleas in Hillsborough, New Hampshire, but on the advice of Gore, who clearly saw bigger and better things for his student, Webster turned it down in order to start his own practice. As a compromise, he moved back to Boscawen and opened an office a few miles from his home.

These were the journeyman years of Webster's career— literally as well as figuratively. He performed a wide range of services, often for little money, and he rode the circuit. His reputation was growing, partly for his work in the courtroom, and also because of the speeches and essays that he produced in these years. It was at this time that Webster began to modify his style and eliminate some of the excessive verbiage that flawed his college speeches. He seems to have done this largely because of the example of Jeremiah Mason, his mentor and frequent competitor in the courtroom. "I owe much to that close attention to the discharge of duties which I was compelled to pay, for nine successive years," he said in a 1848 eulogy for Mason, "from day to day, by Mr. Mason's efforts and arguments at the same bar."[29] Elsewhere he wrote:

Before I went to Portsmouth my style was florid, and I was apt to make longer sentences and to use longer words than were needful. I soon began, however, to notice that Mr. Mason was a cause-getting man. He had a habit of standing quite near to the jury, so near that he might have laid his finger on the foreman's nose, and then he talked to them in a plain conversational way, in short sentences, and using no word that was not level to the comprehension of the least educated man on the panel. This led me to examine my own style, and I set about reforming it altogether.[30]

Webster's other professional interest at this time was politics. The New Hampshire Federalist party was going through a period of changes during these years in response to the energetic Democrat-Republicans who controlled the state (and who were especially dominant in Portsmouth, where Webster moved in 1807). The party worked to repair its diminishing status and to strengthen its organization. One important aspect of this was the rise of the Young Federalists, the second generation of party leaders, to which Webster belonged.[31] Working at local levels to generate support, these tireless young men took to the podium and press with constant industry and occasional flair. Webster's early contributions to this effort consist of two Fryeburg speeches, the anonymous "Appeal to the Old Whigs of New Hampshire," the 1806 Independence Day speech in Concord, and an 1808 attack on the Embargo. All of these works follow a strict

17

Federalist line, praising Washington and Adams while scorn-
ing Jefferson and his ilk as traitors. "Opposition to the Federal
Constitution," wrote Webster in his "Appeal,"

opposition to Washington and Adams, opposition to every important
administration of the federal administration, has invariably been made
by one and the same Party, under different names. Show me a man who
persevered in hostility to the Federal Constitution, and I will show you
a friend of Mr. Jefferson and his administration.[32]

Webster threw himself into politics. He worked very hard
to spread the Federalist message and ran four times for the
state legislature as Portsmouth's representative. In 1812 he
won his first election, becoming Town Moderator—the first
Federalist to hold that position in Portsmouth in over a dozen
years. That summer, the Federal government declared open
war on Britain, and the Federalists stepped up their opposition. A major event in this campaign was the Independence
Day celebration of the Washington Benevolent Society in
Portsmouth. Ostensibly operating as public service organizations, Washington Benevolent Societies existed in many
cities to serve as auxiliaries of the Federalist Party. The choice
of Daniel Webster as principal orator for the 1812 celebration
was a matter of great substance, therefore, an opportunity
for him to speak publicly to a large group of highly motivated
partisans on an occasion that combined politics with social-
izing.

We will consider Webster's speech at length later in this
book; for now we need only note that it was a great success.
An emotional eulogy of Washington and a fiery attack on
the Democrat-Republicans and their policies, the speech asserted the rights of New England to resist not only foreign
(i.e., French) invasion, but also arbitrary commands from
Washington, D.C. Webster's speech made a strong impression
on his listeners. The Portsmouth *Oracle* declared it incom-

parably eloquent,[33] and as a result of this success, the Federalists decided to hold a county meeting to protest the war—the so called Rockingham Convention. Along with roughly two thousand others, Webster attended the protest, and thanks to his performance at Portsmouth, he had the job of writing (not entirely alone, but with the greatest share of responsibility) the convention's manifesto, "The Rockingham Memorial"—a stronger, more sectionalist version of his speech. (In fact, Webster had written the main body of the document before the convention opened.) As a result of his growing fame, Webster received his party's nomination for the 1812 congressional campaign, and, despite Madison's national victory, he won the election.

Webster's first terms in Congress were not especially successful. His sectional and pacifist ideas were decidedly out of step with the militant nationalism championed by Henry Clay and John C. Calhoun, and Webster joined the forces of Timothy Pickering and Christopher Gore (now a senator). An active if minor member of this group, he spent his years sniping at the administration. Opposing trade restrictions, the tariff, the war, enlistments, and conscription, presenting himself very much as a New England man, Webster made many enemies in Washington, although he did increase his standing at home. In the end his chief accomplishment was providing his enemies with ammunition for later recriminations. He did, however, impress everyone with his oratorical presence, and when he left the House in 1817 he had built a solid foundation for a new law practice in Boston.

Webster's career began virtually anew with this move. He turned his full attention to his new family, to establishing himself in Beacon Hill society, and to a growing law practice. In the pattern common for politicians out of office, he was retained by powerful men and firms, his business frequently taking him to Washington. He argued some of the most important United States Supreme Court cases of this time, and they all helped him to move towards an increasingly stong position in favor of centralized government. *Dartmouth College v. Woodward, McCulloch v. Maryland, Gibbon v. Ogden,* and other cases may have differed in particulars, but they all involved the general definition of Federal and state powers.

Success in constitutional cases on behalf of corporations, banks, and businessmen made aristocratic Boston even more fond of Webster than his politics already had. He simultaneously gained a high reputation among the state's voters, chiefly as a result of his oratorical abilities: his dramatic advocacy in cases such as the defense of the Kennistons (a trial followed by the press as a thrilling mystery beautifully managed and presented by Webster) and a single occasional address, "The First Settlement of New England."

Webster took time out from his duties as leader of the Massachusetts Constitutional Convention in December 1820 to address the Pilgrim Society of Plymouth on the bicentennial of the Pilgrim's landing. Under the auspices of various organizations, Plymouth had hosted such celebrations since 1769; more often than not, the keynote addresses were sermons. Webster, his fame on the rise, drew an audience of about twelve hundred persons to hear his two-hour-long speech. Attired in formal dress—silk stockings and gown and buckled shoes—Webster stood before the crowd an impressive and dramatic figure. Intertwining history with political digressions and prophecies for the future, Webster virtually created in that speech the legend of the Pilgrim Fathers. It was a tremendous performance, one described notably by George Ticknor:

I was never so excited by public speaking before in my life. Three or four times I thought my temples would burst with the gush of blood; for, after all, you must know that I am aware that it is no connected and compacted whole, but a collection of wonderful fragments of burning

20

eloquence, to which his manner gave ten-fold force. When I came out, I was almost afraid to come near him. It seemed to me as if he was like the mount that might not be touched and that burned with fire. I was beside myself and am so still.[34]

Like the "Address before the Washington Benevolent Society," this Pilgrim speech stimulated Webster's career wonderfully. He had helped to create the nation's legal character in the courts; at Plymouth on that cold December afternoon, Webster gave New England a sense of itself in spiritual and historic terms. Webster provided for Massachusetts and its neighbors a renewed sense of its past and future. He vowed that his listeners would know and fulfill their mission as the true founders of the nation:

We would leave for the consideration of those who shall occupy our places, some proof that we hold these blessings transmitted from our fathers in just estimation; some proof of our attachment to the cause of good government, and of civil and religious liberty; some proof of a sincere and ardent desire to promote every thing which may enlarge the understandings and improve the hearts of men.[35]

Webster gave New Englanders pride in their origins and in the tasks that he outlined for them, making himself a natural spokesman for the region and an obvious choice two years later when a group of leading Bostonians sought a strong popular candidate to run for Congress. William Sturgis called on Webster: "I come to ask you to throw down your lawbooks," he told the once and future congressman, "and enter the service of the public; for to the public you belong."[36] Webster heard the call, accepted his party's nomination, and handily won election to the House of Representatives.

This reincarnated congressional career began much more auspiciously than did the first. Even while Federalism was dying as a national party, Webster adapted well to the changing political situation. A rebel during the war years, he had since become one of the strongest supporters of the

21

central government. Despite the ominous sectionalism that had marked the Missouri debate, nationalistic sentiments were high when Webster returned to the Capitol. One expression of this was a tremendous popular interest in supporting the Greek rebellion against Turkey. As a projection of American pride, this cause was a very safe issue with favor on all partisan sides. Knowing that even President Monroe had spoken favorably of the Greeks, and seeking a chance to make a big speech that perhaps, as others had, would bring him attention and power, Webster decided to speak on the matter.

Webster seems to have known rather little about Greece, but with the help of Edward Everett (professor of Greek literature at Harvard, and aspirant to become United States Ambassador to Greece), he assembled a considerable amount of information. On December 8, 1823, Webster introduced a resolution to provide funds for a Presidential commissioner. The motion eventually failed, but Webster profited from his opportunistic efforts. "The Revolution in Greece," delivered in support of his measure, resembled "The First Settlement of New England," and was Webster's first spectacular Washington rhetorical success. Recalling the importance of Greece to all representative governments, Webster called on America to speak for the spirit of the times. Only the United States could lead the world into the future, and only by opposing the Holy Alliance of Russia, Austria, and Prussia that sought to return the world to the dark ages. Just as the Pilgrim speech had given New England a sense of identity and mission, so did this address have a similar effect for the entire country. Capturing the enormous popular excitement for Greece, Webster inspired Americans:

The age is extraordinary; the spirit that actuates it is peculiar and marked; and our own relation to the times we live in, and to the questions which interest them, is equally marked and peculiar. We are placed, by our good fortune and the wisdom and valor of our ancestors, in a condition in which we *can* act no obsure part.[37]

Webster may have been speaking about Greece, but that subject was only his pretext for celebrating his own country as the new power for the new age.

Webster delivered some of his best and most powerful speeches in this decade, especially in the way of occasional addresses. Along with "The First Settlement of New England" (and perhaps "The Revolution in Greece" as well, which despite its Capitol setting resembled a public oration more than it did a legislative one), Webster gave "The Bunker Hill Monument" in 1825 and his splendid eulogy, "Adams and Jefferson" the next year.

Through the rest of the decade, Webster spoke on a variety of subjects, but those four years were relatively quiet ones for him—all of which ended in the nullification debate. The Missouri Compromise had only postponed confrontation between the North and South, and in fact probably excited rather than soothed sectional tensions. Discussions of the new tariff in 1828 helped spur the quarrel. John C. Calhoun had supported the Tariff of 1824, but fearing that protective taxes would help the North to the ultimate detriment of Southern agriculture, he succumbed to sectionalism even as Webster was becoming more nationalistic. Attempts to weaken the tariff only resulted in making it stronger in 1828, leading to the so-called Tariff of Abominations. Although he ran as Jackson's Vice Presidential candidate that year, Calhoun would take no more of what he considered abuses of Federal power. He wrote and published anonymously *The South Carolina Exposition and Protest* in which he explained his theory of nullification. Calhoun's arguments resembled in spirit those used by Webster in his own resistance to Federal decisions on the Embargo and War of 1812. Assuming that the parties to the creation of the government retained their sovereignty and could excercise it at will, Calhoun insisted that each state had the right to judge the constitutionality of Federal laws. Should a state legislature deem an act in violation of the spirit or letter of the Constitution, that state could vote to nullify and then legally ignore the act.

Expecting Jackson to ease the offending tariff, South Carolina did not actually vote to nullify it until November, 1832. But the issue came to the Senate in early 1830 as part of a debate over policy regarding land in the West. Senators Benton of Missouri and Hayne of South Carolina accused the North of trying to suppress the West, which region they expected to ally itself with the South. Webster, whom Massachusetts had transferred to the Senate in 1827, responded to Hayne briefly but pointedly. He limited his reply mainly to defending New England against Hayne's slurs, but also included some provoking comments about South Carolina's recent attitude towards the rest of the Union. An accomplished debater who foolishly fancied Webster an easy mark, Hayne raised the stakes. His second speech is a masterpiece of invective, attacking not only New England and Massachusetts but Webster himself. Nor surprisingly, Hayne charged Webster with inconsistency on the tariff (which Webster had fought in 1816 then supported in 1828) and on Federal-state relations. Hayne closed with a formidable presentation of the nullification doctrine.

Webster's "Second Reply to Hayne" (also known as the "Second Speech on Foot's Resolution")[38] was the most important statement that Webster ever made on the Constitution and Union. We will look at the speech in detail later; for now, we should note that although Webster's speech did not end nullification or even prevent eventual attempts at secession, it was nevertheless a powerful personal success for Webster.

Reaction was not immediate. The Senate sat silently for a few moments until Vice President Calhoun adjourned it after Webster's closing words. In the next few days and weeks, though, letters and gifts began to arrive from citizens who had read the speech in its printed form throughout the nation. The pamphlet edition of the speech sold phenomenally well: reporting the printing of nearly 40,000 copies by his own press and of twenty other editions across the country, Joseph Gales of the Washington *National Intelligencer* wrote, "It is hardly too much to say, that no speech in the English language has ever been so universally diffused, or so generally read."[39] With a single speech—actually almost with only the two paragraph peroration—Daniel Webster became one of the country's most prominent leaders. Banquets and celebrations in his honor multiplied. "We are now arrived," wrote Ticknor Curtis of the transformation that this speech worked so suddenly on Webster's life, " at the period . . . when he began to be considered by a part of the people in the North and the West, and by many in the South, . . . the most suitable person to be brought forward as a candidate for the presidency."[40]

Webster began at once to capitalize on his new reputation as the Defender of the Constitution and the Slayer of Nullification. During the rest of the crisis (which lasted until Congress passed a genuine compromise tariff in 1833), he steered a careful course. With good reasons, he considered himself a likely presidential contender in a new party that he imagined might be formed with Jackson—a Union party drawing from both Democrats and National Republicans. For the next several years, Webster delivered a number of occasional addresses supporting the Constitution and, by a happy coincidence, keeping himself before the. voters.

The second major conflict of the Jackson administration affected Webster's career in exactly the opposite way that nullification did. Frightened of banks in general and of Nicholas Biddle's Second Bank of the United States in particular, President Jackson determined to destroy that institution in a move to decentralize economic power. He vetoed the Bank's renewal and ordered removal of Federal funds from its accounts. On retainer to Biddle and convinced of the Bank's merits, Webster tried to stay neutral for a time, but eventually joined the fight against Jackson. Hopes of a new party collapsed.

Webster's immediate presidential ambitions were doomed. At the very height of his career and national "availability," he found himself pilloried as a paid lackey of the Bank. His dreams of putting together an alliance with Jackson over, Webster ended up as a disappointed partner with Henry Clay in the embryonic association of old Federalists, National Republicans, disaffected Jacksonians, and other scattered interest groups. Calling Jackson "King Andrew," the new party claimed ideological descent from the American Revolutionaries. For a long time, the Whig party was considered nothing more than an amalgamation of opportunists with nothing in common other than their opposition to Jackson. Daniel Walker Howe in his *The Political Culture of the American Whigs* presents a different analysis of the party. Howe argues persuasively that a coherent if diverse set of principles characterized the Whigs. In general they supported the Bank, a protective tariff, mixed currency, public education, "reform," and a strong federal government dominated by the legislative branch. Whigs opposed nullification, slavery (although they recognized constitutional guarantees of it in the South), expansionistic wars, a strong executive, and most anything that the Democrats supported.[41]

Hoping to repeat the circumstances of 1824 and force the presidential election into the House of Representatives, the Whigs ran three presidential candidates in 1836: Hugh White,

William Henry Harrison, and Daniel Webster. The strategy failed: Martin Van Buren won 170 electoral votes to the 113 split by the three Whigs. Webster won only 14 electors, representing only 2.7 percent of the popular vote. His first foray into presidential politics had failed utterly. His image as a New England man and as a friend to the wealthy undercut his attractiveness to an electorate growing increasingly proletarian.

Still in the opposition party, Webster spent 1837 decrying Democratic policies, especially in regard to financial matters. The year 1835 had seen the end of the national debt and the beginning of easy credit. The resulting boom brought speculation, inflation, and currency troubles. These and other factors led to the Panic of 1837, in which some banks failed and others hoarded specie. Webster summed up the situation hyperbolically yet fairly accurately when he told a St. Louis audience that year, " Neither people nor government can fulfill its contract. All are broke."[42] Van Buren's four years as President must have been miserable, and Webster did nothing to ease the President's distress. He fought his policies and criticized him whenever he could. Partly in an effort to overcome his reputation as a friend of Biddle and the rich, Webster delivered frequent speeches in these years on behalf of the common man, whose life he portrayed in collapse while Van Buren and his ilk enjoyed a high standard of living at the nation's expense.

Apart from his work on the economy, Webster's chief activities during Van Buren's tenure involved foreign affairs. The Maine Controversy, reviving a boundary dispute from 1783, interested him. Congress recommended that Van Buren send Webster as negotiating delegate to London, but the President (whose own nomination to be Ambassador to the Court of St. James Webster had helped kill years earlier) refused to go along. Denied a ministerial commission, Webster resolved to visit Britain in a private capacity.

The trip was a splendid success. Wherever he went, Webster found himself welcomed and acclaimed. He met the political leaders, was presented to Queen Victoria, and dined with Wordsworth, Macauley, and Dickens. Thomas Carlyle wrote a famous letter to Emerson:

Not many days ago I saw at breakfast the notablest of your notables, Daniel Webster. He is a magnificent specimen. You might say to all the world, "This is our Yankee Englishman; such limbs we make in Yankee land!" As a logic-fancier, advocate, or parliamentary Hercules, one would incline to back him against all the extant world. The tanned complexion; that amorphous, craglike face; the dull black eyes under the precipice of brows, like dull anthracite furnaces needing only to be *blown;* the mastiff mouth, accurately closed; I have not traced so much of the *silent Berserker rage* that I remember of, in any other man . . . Webster is not loquacious, but he is pertinent, conclusive; a dignified, perfectly-bred man, though not English in breeding; a man worthy of the best reception among us, and meeting such, I understand.[43]

To his hosts, Webster seemed the powerful spirit of America personified. All the words of Ralph Waldo Emerson could not explain America as well as a single visit by the Champion of the Union.

Webster returned to the United States in late 1839, ready for the next year's campaign. Having already withdrawn his own name from contention, he was surprised when Henry Clay did not receive the nomination. Seeking a winner, the Whigs recalled that Harrison had led their pack in 1836, and chose him in 1840. That campaign represents something of a political downfall for the United States. Frustrated by the Democrats for a dozen years, the Whigs would do almost anything to win. Following the example of Jackson's 1828 campaign, Harrison ran on a populist image with the strikingly named Thurlow Weed as his campaign manager. He appeared before voters as a simple man born in a log cabin and raised to power and fame only through his courage and virtue. Out-Democrating the Democrats, the Whigs characterized Van Buren (who had much more humble origins that Harrison) as an aristocrat squandering taxes on personal luxuries while the people suffered from his foolish ideas.

Drawing on the same tropes that he used to attack Van Buren over fiscal policies, Webster came out strongly in favor of Harrison. He stumped the country for his party's cause, speaking some of the most awkward rhetoric that he would ever use. Gone were the grand sweep and extensive narratives of the thirties. Instead Webster gave brief scenes and vignettes, trite exercises in propaganda designed to make him and his candidate look every inch commoners. "I come today to hear the sentiments of the people of Suffolk County on those topics that agitate the times," he declared to an audience in Patchogue, New York,

I am much too old to make an oratorical speech. I am too old for that! If, my friends, there have been times and occasions in the course of my past career in which I might have wished to display of anything like oratory, that time is far gone by.

But although I do not wish to do this, yet I have opinions upon the present state of things, and I come to speak those opinions plainly to you, and to hear yours in return. I come to make no flourishes of figures, but to make a plain speech to the intelligence of this country.[44]

This change in Webster's speech patterns is a striking one, inspired in part by his failures in the thirties and a desire, no doubt, to get on the democratic bandwagon by refuting his earlier "oratorical" sophistication. It never rings true, though; Webster always sounds at odds with himself.

The strategy worked for the Whigs, however, and for his efforts Webster was named Secretary of State when Harrison took office. With a weak President and lesser men as his colleagues in the Cabinet, Webster promised to be the real power in the administration. He imagined following Harrison into the White House in a few years. All of this depended, of course, on a compliant chief executive—which the party lost when Harrison died soon after his inauguration. The discordant nature of the Whig alliance showed itself at once when John Tyler took office. Chosen to attract Southern votes, Tyler belonged to the Whigs mainly because he hated Jackson. A strong supporter of states' rights, Tyler opposed the Bank, the tariff, and nearly all of the other principles of his nominal party. He and Webster had for years quarreled in the Senate on almost every matter possible.

Clay despised Tyler and insisted that as the guiding genius of the Whigs he would dominate the administration. The President and the Senator came into conflict almost at once over the Bank, with Clay supporting it as usual and Tyler sounding remarkably like Andrew Jackson. The resulting rift in the party left Webster in an awkward position. He tried to make peace between Clay and Tyler, but when the latter continued to veto the Bank in any form, Webster suddenly discovered himself the only original Cabinet officer who would stay by the President. On September 11, 1841, the others all resigned in protest. A sense of duty to Tyler both as a man and as the head of the government—and perhaps a stubborn resistance to Clay—kept Webster in the State Department. He defended his decision on the grounds that it helped party unity, speaking of "the whole party, the Whig President, the Whig Congress, and the Whig people."[45] No matter how well he might have meant, though, Webster's show of loyalty did little good for anyone—least of all for himself. Clay and his followers pronounced Tyler (and, by association, Webster) anathema.

Webster stayed with Tyler for nearly two more years. As Secretary of State he concentrated on Anglo-American relations, in which his familiarity with the Maine question and friendship with British leaders helped him in negotiations with Lord Ashburton in 1842. Using an old map that favored the British, Webster urged mutual concessions. He and Ashburton concluded a compromise that both governments approved, the Treaty of Washington, which, along with ancillary agreements, put to rest a number of nagging problems between England and the United States. As Secretary of State, Webster had reason for pride and happiness.

As a Whig, however, Webster had less cause for ease. Even though he did eventually break with Tyler, his party still mistrusted him. No longer the brilliant young man of promise, Webster now found enemies even among Massachusetts Whigs. Abbot Lowell Lawrence, once a supporter of Webster, wrote to him in July, 1842, "I have deliberately considered the consequences that would result to yourself, of delay in this delicate matter [i.e., leaving the administration] . . . I shall, therefore, without stating the reasons that operate on my mind, recommend to you, after our treaty should have been signed, to give notice at once, to the President." To make his meaning perfectly clear, Lawrence added, "[Y]our *real* friends, I think, will unanimously agree that *now* is the *accepted* time to quit."[46] The Whig party underscored Lawrence's message on September 17th when it declared that Tyler no longer belonged to the Whig party. The unkindest cut of all for Webster came when the Massachusetts Whigs nominated Henry Clay to run for the Presidency.

Invited to a small dinner in Boston and expected to lay his sword at Lawrence's feet, Webster insisted that he would appear only at a public gathering at Faneuil Hall. On September 30, he addressed those out to break him and left no doubt about his convictions. "I am a Whig," he said, "I have always been a Whig, and I will always be one; and if there are any who would turn me out of the pale of that common, let them see who will get out first." He continued,

I am a Massachusettes Whig, a Faneuil Hall Whig, having breathed this air for five-and-twenty years, and meaning to breathe it, as long as my life is spared. I am ready to submit to all decisions of Whig conventions on subjects on which they are authorized to make decisions; I know that great party good and great public good can only be so obtained. But it is quite another question whether a set of gentlemen, however respectable they may be as individuals, shall have the power to bind me on matters which I have not agreed to submit to their decision at all.[47]

Webster considered this the final word. Events in Washington made his resolve to stand by Tyler impossible, though, as the President worked for the admission of Texas as a slave state. Webster finally left his post in May, 1843 to return to Boston and resume his political life. As he had in the past, Webster sought to renew his fortunes by speaking. He chose an issue with national interest—the tariff—and went out onto the road. Despite his earlier support of tariffs, Webster now drew on his considerable expertise in diplomacy to call for international trade agreements, especially in an attempt to foster good relations between potential enemies. He seems to have had in mind building support for himself as a Presidential candidate in 1844. He spoke to large crowds, including one assembled at Bunker Hill for the completion of the monument that he had celebrated years earlier. As personal promotion, the plan failed. Webster rejoined the Whigs by the end of the year and let it be known that he would support Henry Clay if the party chose him. Webster did salvage something from the wreckage, though: his candidate, George Briggs, beat Abbot Lowell Lawrence for the Whig gubernatorial nomination in Massachusetts.

Webster worked ardently for Clay. The campaign of 1844 resembled that of 1840 in that the party characterized it as a revolution against an abusive executive. Travelling throughout the northeast, Webster claimed for Clay the mantle of George Washington, making the contest part of a continuing history of American freedom fighting. James K. Polk he called a radical who would—as he had said of the Jeffersonians decades earlier—overthrow the legacy of the Founding Fathers. Fearing the unbalancing effects of expansion, Webster criticized Polk above all for his plan to annex Texas. "The question is," he told a Boston audience, "Polk and Texas, or no Polk and no Texas."[48] Texas for Webster meant slavery, sectional division, and war. Clay might well have won the election had he not prevaricated on Texas, but in trying to please Southern voters he spoiled his chances by alienating free-soilers in the North. Clay lost by 38,000 out of 2,700,000 popular votes. When the dust settled, Webster had won his way back to the leadership of the Whigs. With his clumsy defeat, Clay had effectively ruled himself out as a future candidate. Amazingly in light of all that had passed since 1840, Webster had finessed himself a good chance at the 1848 nomination. He returned to the Senate in December, 1845, with his prospects much improved.

When Polk took office, he vowed to lower the tariff, restore the Independent Treasury, curtail Federally funded internal improvements, and increase the Union by adding Oregon, Texas, and other territory. Webster opposed each of these, losing out to Polk on every one, and he also spent these years working hard to keep Whigs united. Although still the leading Whig in Massachusetts, he had to reckon with a new generation of men, the Young Whigs, who had no time for his compromises. Charles Sumner, Charles Francis Adams, and others demanded that Webster speak out for abolition. Webster despised slavery, but he refused to risk a break between Northern and Southern Whigs by backing what he considered an extreme and unconstitutional position. Cries for action persisted, though, despite Webster's pleas for calm.

The Polk administration was a terrible time for Daniel Webster. In a difficult position as a leader of an increasingly polarized party, he found his moderation under attack in

Washington as well as in Massachusetts. Since 1843 his foes had charged him with being overly generous to the British in regard to the Maine-Canada border. When the Oregon question arose and Webster urged a peaceful settlement of its disputed boundary, opponents intensified their criticism under the leadership of Democrats such as Charles Ingersoll and William Yancey. These men brought informal and formal charges against Webster.

Ingersoll, who had hated Webster since they had disagreed over the war of 1812, suggested that he had tried to influence William Seward, then governor of New York, regarding a Canadian citizen who had been arrested for the murder of an American. Webster fired back in anger. Ingersoll then charged that Webster had used government money to buy the support of newspapers that endorsed the treaty. All hell broke loose: friends and enemies of Webster railed on the Hill and in the press. Webster soon faced not only Ingersoll's charges, but also a new indictment from Yancey that he had accepted bribes from Massachusetts industrialists.

Both charges had some truth to them. Friends and supporters in Boston *had* set up an annuity for Webster, ostensibly to provide for his retirement. Expensive tastes and the demands that public service made on his time kept Webster in debt; the annuity was a gift to thank and to help the Senator. Of course, Webster's gratitude in return was certainly likely to benefit those who had been so generous. Little came of Yancey's accusations, however. In the end, Congress did not investigate Webster's behavior; Ingersoll's assertions were finally dismissed by a House committee, but only after John Tyler said that he had authorized spending the money in question for "the employment of confidential agents."[49]

Formally acquitted, Webster nevertheless suffered from all this. An air of corruption hung about him despite his evident innocence. Along with the substantive charges, Webster had been reviled as a lifelong Anglophile. Recalling his resistance to the the War of 1812, Yancey and his friends claimed not only that Webster had tried to deny needed supplies to American troops, but that he had even suggested that New England might secede to form an alliance with the British. These attacks came at an especially bad time for Webster: Polk had just started a war with Mexico, a war that Webster opposed on every possible ground. With Yancey stirring up excitement about his pacifism, Webster felt pinched. For a while he only went so far as to urge that no new territory be added to the Union as a result of the war. Eventually, though, Webster came out more definitely against the enterprise. Speaking to Springfield Whigs, he called it "most unnecessary, and therefore most unjustifiable." Yancey's accusations doubtless helped inspire his words:

I honor those who are called upon, by professional duty, to bear arms in their country's cause, and do their duty well. I would obscure none of their fame. But I will say here, and to them, that it is the solemn adjudication of nations, and it is the sentiment of the Christian world, that a war waged for vicious purposes, or from vicious motives, tarnishes the luster of arms; and darkens, if it does not blot, what other wise might be a glorious page in the history of the nation that makes it.[50]

In its war against Mexico, America betrayed the promise that Webster had celebrated in speeches for decades: instead of leading the world in peace and diplomacy, the republic stooped to conquest.

All was calamity for Webster in these years. Two of his children died—his favorite son's body arrived back from the Mexican War on the day of his daughter's funeral. Assailed from all sides and losing every fight, Webster saw his presidential hopes fade along with other happiness. A tour of the South in 1847 ended early because of illness and his recognition of the trip's futility as a campaign effort. With opportunistic zeal even more transparent than it had shown in 1840, the Whigs rallied around General Zachary Taylor, the Hero of Buena Vista. Webster could bring himself to say but one thing in Taylor's favor: "He is the only Whig candidate before the people, and the only Whig candidate who can receive any vote for the office of the President."[51] In what it meant to his family, his principles, his work in the Senate, and his own plans, the Mexican War nearly crushed Webster.

With the balance of free and slave states equal in the Senate, the country faced a new fight over how to treat the territory acquired from Mexico. A slaveholder himself, Taylor believed that the Constitution would prevent an abolitionist majority in Congress from interfering with slavery, and he expected the new states to enter peacefully regardless of their stand on involuntary servitude. The Democratically dominated Congress disagreed. The House was already badly divided. During a long battle to choose its Speaker, the chamber shook with cries for disunion and civil war. Threats of personal violence replaced debate until, at last, a compromise put a Georgia Democrat in the lead over Robert Winthrop, a Massachusetts man. To this Congress, Taylor sent his first annual message, blithely urging that California join the Union at once and that future states be allowed to enter as well; the matter of slavery was not taken into account. California had already proclaimed itself free, and New Nexico showed signs of doing the same, so Taylor's advice fired anew the barely quieted fight. Free-soilers fell in line with Taylor; Southern leaders planned the Nashville Convention to protect their interests.

Apart from the years of the War of 1812, Webster had preached the inviolability of the Union for five decades. No matter how much he disliked slavery, Webster would not put the country on the line to abolish it. He knew full well how strongly his Northern constituents felt about slavery, but he still believed in the possibility of conciliation. Belea-guered and hopeful that the crisis would pass, Webster sat silently while Clay proposed a series of compromise measures intended to end the strife once and for all. In exchange for California's admission as a free state and the abolition of slave trade in Washington, D.C., the South would receive a promise that slavery would be left alone and that a new Fugitive Slave Law would be strictly enforced—even in places like Boston, where resistance would run strong. Clay intro-duced his resolutions on January 29, 1850 after consulting Webster to seek his old rival's support. The Senator from Massachusetts agreed, promising Clay that he would help no matter what it might mean for his personal fortunes.

Webster did nothing for over a month, perhaps hoping that the Compromise of 1850 would succeed without any sacrifices on his part. As the fight grew more heated, though, he prepared to enter the debate. Tired, embattled, his skill as a speaker rusted by too many mediocre efforts since his great days, Webster wrote to a friend, "I mean to make a Union speech."[52] Following Calhoun's powerful secessionist attack on the North (which, due to the illness that would soon kill Calhoun, was read by another), Webster rose on the seventh day of March. "I wish to speak today," he began, "not as a Massachusetts man, nor as a Northern man, but as an American, a member of the Senate of the United States. . . . I have a duty to perform and I mean to perform it with fidelity, not without a sense of existing dangers, but not without hope."[53]

Tracing the history of slavery in the United States, Webster analyzed the current problem. He blamed extremists on both sides, chastising the North in particular. Abolition contra-dicted the constitutional guarantees that protected slavery; free-soil demands only gave rhetorical ammunition to South-erners threatening secession and war. Webster's main point was that no one had any right "in their legislative capacity or in any other capacity, to endeavor to get round the Constitution, or to embarrass the free exercise of the rights secured by the Constitution to the persons whose slaves escape from them." (vol. 10, p. 97). No matter what he or others might prefer, the Constitution prevented interference with slavery. To ensure the legal rights of slaveholders, Webster vowed to support the Fugitive Slave Law.

Webster's speech went over well in the West and South, but Northerners took it less happily. To strengthen his position (and to prevent splits in the Massachusetts party), Webster arranged for friends to get up a letter of support signed by hundreds of prominent Bostonians. He himself considered it "probably the most important effort of my life."[54] With his aid, over 200,000 copies were printed and distributed. Nonetheless, criticism began in earnest. Free-soilers held a meeting in Faneuil Hall in which they savaged Webster. Responding to the speech two weeks after its delivery, Theodore Parker refused to grant precedence to the Union over freedom for slaves. To his eyes, Webster had not taken a bold step for the sake of the country; rather, he had sold himself and betrayed the promise of his youth:

Mr. Webster has spoken noble words—at Plymouth, standing on the altar-stone of New England; at Bunker Hill, the spot so early reddened with the blood of our fathers. But at this hour, when we looked for great counsel, when we forgot the paltry things which he has after-done, and said, "Now he will rouse his noble soul, and be the man his early speeches once bespoke," who dared to fear that Olympian head would bow so low, so deeply kiss the ground?[55]

Wendell Phillips was unconvinced as well by Webster's pro-Constitution arguments. "Who can blame us for detesting that Moloch Constitution," he asked, "to which the fair face of our statesman is sacrificed?"[56] And Emerson, who once considered Webster the epitome of his age and nation, wrote,

"Mr. Webster is a man who lives by his memory, a man of the past, not a man of faith and hope."[57] Webster's oratory had brought him more criticism than ever before.

The accession of Millard Fillmore to the presidency after Taylor's death and Webster's own appointment as Secretary of State by Fillmore gave him a false sense of confidence. Not only was he the most powerful member of a pro-Compromise administration, but he also seemed a likely candidate for the Whig nomination in 1852. Webster believed that the furor would end soon, and he dreamed again of the formation of a new Union party. "I can sleep now nights," he wrote to Peter Harvey in October, 1850,

We have gone through the most important crisis, which has occurred since the foundation of the Government: & whatever party may prevail, hereafter, the Union stands firm. . . . Another thing is not altogether improbable. And that is a remodelling of Parties. If any considerable body of Whigs of the North shall get in the spirit of the majority of the recent convention in N. York, a new arrangement of Parties is inavoidable. There must be a Union Party, and an opposing party under some name, I know not what, very likely the Party of Liberty.[58]

In fact, the crisis that Webster wanted to dismiss grew worse all along. Furious citizens came out to prevent enforcement of the Fugitive Slave Law; several incidents occurred in Boston. Webster persisted, however, in looking for a bright side. Traveling around the country in a remarkable public relations tour, he tried to revive the spirit of unity and promise that he had celebrated twenty years earlier during the nullification crisis. Desperate in their forced optimism, these speeches contrast with their earier counterparts, although they contain some fine passages. Swearing that Massachusetts would return to the fold, Webster claimed that the future looked golden. Even as he spoke, abolitionists grew more powerful and Webster's vision of America proved increasingly unrealistic. He continued on his old straight course, but many of those who once would have followed refused.

Hoping to divert the country's attention and to rally support for a safe issue as he had done with his speech on the Greek rebellion in 1824, Webster took part in the Kossuth Affair, which involved a leader in the Hungarian revolt against Austria. Webster supported Kossuth with strong words directed against Austria, but backed down rather suddenly when Kossuth arrived in America and proved something of a charlatan. Neither Webster's hopeful words about the Union nor the distraction of Hungary solved the problems besetting him and the country.

Webster retained a significant national following in spite of his troubles, though, and he entered the campaign of 1852 with expectations of success. He had fallen too low among his old partisans, though, and his ideal Unionism was out of date. Denied his party's nomination, Webster did receive the endorsement of an inconsequential splinter group, the Georgia Whigs, but he won only a very few votes.

Webster spent the next four months largely at his Marshfield estate. He refused to endorse Scott, saying nothing at all in public while quietly praising Democrat Franklin Pierce to friends. Ill since the spring, Webster began to plan for his death. He composed an epitaph, ordered a flag flown within sight of his bed, and gathered his family and remaining friends around him. On October 23, 1852, he slipped in and out of consciousness and died quietly. Near the end, his sense of himself as a man of words persisting even to the grave, he awoke to ask, "Have I,—wife, son, doctor, friends, are you all here?—have I, on this occasion, said anything unworthy of Daniel Webster?[59]

2. The Aesthetic of History

The language that Webster used, both his diction and the rhetorical strategies in his speeches, had a formal kinship with the theories and practices of literature that marked nineteenth-century American learned culture. Although he gave up a life of letters per se when he entered politics and the law, Webster never really abandoned the poetic instincts and inclinations that he developed as a child and young man. Very occasionally, he spoke or wrote about his craft, revealing how he looked on rhetoric not simply as a useful skill, but as an imaginative and highly creative art. As Webster perceived his speeches, imaginative language was a crucial element of political communication.

As a student at Dartmouth at the beginning of the Romantic era of literature, Webster studied and put into practice the new ideas about language that were coming from Britain. We cannot with perfect surety reconstruct Webster's reading, but we can assume that he read—and that as Librarian he perhaps purchased—the most prominent of the new works on language and oratory. These included Locke's *Essay on Human Understanding* with its insights into faculty psychology, Hugh Blair's *Lectures on Rhetoric and Belles-Lettres,* Lord Kames' *The Elements of Criticism,* Archibald Alison's *Essays on the Nature and Principles of Taste,* George Campbell's *The Philosophy of Rhetoric,* Dugald Stewart's *Elements of the Philosophy of the Human Mind,* Thomas Reid's *An Inquiry into the Human Mind,* Charles Rollin's *The Method of Teaching and Studying the Belles Lettres,* and a number of other topical works that marked and helped to inspire the revolution in language and literature associated with the rise of Romanticism in America as well as abroad.[1]

Already possessing a trained instinct for oratory, Webster learned a great deal from these authors about how to move audiences with persuasive language. The most important works centered around or derived from the relatively new school of faculty psychology. Drawing on the work of John Locke—whose *Essay on Human Understanding* was one of the most well-read books at Dartmouth[2]—this paradigm of the human mind split the psyche into two parts: Understanding and Will. Rather than accepting the notion that logic and reason govern our behavior, faculty psychology insisted that appeals to the Understanding (the "logical" part of the mind) were not sufficient to stir a person to action. Adherents of this theory believed that the Will (or the emotional half) was the truly effective avenue to persuasion. Obviously, this complicated theory is quite commonsensical; when Marc Antony reconstructed Brutus' cold and dispassionate discourse in order to incite the Roman mob, he was practicing the rhetorical teachings associated with faculty psychology.

A survey of all of Webster's likely reading on language is beyond the scope of this book, but a few observations about one especially representative and popular work will give us a taste of the critical foundations of his life in language. Webster definitely knew Lord Kames' *The Elements of Criticism*, a popular book listed among the requirements for admission to the status of Junior at Dartmouth. Kames began his study of language with a long consideration of human feelings. We find chapters on the "Power of Sounds to raise Emotions and Passions" and the "Sympathetic Emotion of Virtue, and its cause." And in a section entitled "Emotions caused by Fiction," Kames revealed a utilitarian streak. "[P]assions, as all the world know, are moved by fiction as well by truth," wrote Kames; "I shall take occasion afterward to show, that the power of fiction to generate passion is an admirable contrivance, subservient to excellent purposes."[3] Kames argued that fiction affected our emotions by virtue of its "ideal presence," which he contrasted with "real presence" and defined as

a *waking dream;* because, like a dream, it vanisheth the moment we reflect upon our present situation: real presence, on the contrary, vouched by eye-sight, commands our belief, not only during the direct perception, but in reflecting afterward on the object. To distinguish ideal presence from reflective remembrance, I give the following illustration: when I think of an event as past, without forming any image, it is barely reflecting or remembering that I was an eye-witness: but when I recall the event so distinctly as to form a complete image of it, I perceive it as passing in my presence; and this perception is an act of intuition, into which reflection enters not, more than into an act of sight.[4]

Ideal presence, in other words, is the imaginative recreation of a previous reality—or, as Kames made clear, the veritable *creation* of something very akin to reality in terms of how the mind works and is influenced. It is an essential part of communication, he insisted:

> It is wonderful to observe, upon what slight foundations nature erects some of her most solid and magnificent works. In appearance at least, what can be more slight than ideal presence? And yet from it is derived that extensive influence which language hath over the heart; an influence, which, more than any other means, strengthens the bonds of society, and attracts individuals from their private system to perform acts of generosity and benevolence. Matters of fact, it is true, and truth in general, may be inculcated without taking advantage of ideal presence; but without it, the finest speaker or writer would in vain attempt to move any passion. . . . Nor is the influence of language, by means of ideal presence, confined to the heart: it reaches also the understanding, and contributes to belief. For when events are related in a lively manner, and every circumstance appears as passing before us, we suffer not patiently the truth of the facts to be questioned. An historian accordingly who hath a genius for narration, seldom fails to engage our belief.[5]

Later in his book Kames argued that persons dealing in history ought to avoid too much "ideal presence," but the clear lesson of his work is that the most moving kind of language plays upon the passions, and that it does so by resembling fiction. The utilitarian significance of this would be clear to Webster and his fraternity brothers in their efforts to become more persuasive speakers.

Webster was by far the outstanding orator on campus in his day. A competent if not brilliant student in his formal classes, he excelled on the podium. The Reverend Elihu Smith, classmate, left a vivid description of the delivery style that would characterize Webster throughout his life. "In his movements, he was rather slow and deliberate," wrote Smith, "except when his feelings were aroused; then, his whole soul would kindle into a flame. I recollect that he used to commence speaking rather monotonously and without much excitement, but would always rise, with the importance of the subject, till every eye was fixed upon him."[6] (Not everyone loved Webster with equal ardor. Aaron Loveland, his roommate, found "something rather amusing and pompous in his bearing as well as his style. He was, and felt himself to be a kind of oracle;" Loveland recalled him as "very ambitious in college from the first, and took every opportunity to make himself conspicuous. He had unbounded self-confidence, seemed to feel that a good deal belonged to him, and evidently intended to be a great man in public life."[7])

Dressed in fine Federalist attire of silk gloves and velvet trousers—all charged on account in what would be a lifetime's habit of relying on credit—Webster spoke on several special occasions during his years at Dartmouth. On the Fourth of July, 1800, the citizens of Hanover and the surrounding area gathered to hear his maiden public speech at their invitation. This short address by the nineteen-year-old college junior embarrasses most Webster biographers in comparison with his later "true" work. As a good example of Webster's style throughout his early years, though, it deserves consideration. Although the particular phrasings and figures little resemble the language that Webster would use in his mature speeches, the rhetorical strategies of this speech proved quite persistent. It is a speech filled with "ideal presence," relying on fictive and poetic devices to convey its substance. We might look at the talk as consisting of three categories of information: issues, themes, and motifs. Issues are the particular historical matters the merit of which Webster wants to convince his audience. Themes comprise the broader ideological framework.[8] Webster's issues in the Hanover address are simple and straightforward: he wants to support the Federalist John Adams in his approaching presidential campaign against Thomas Jefferson, and to avoid any closeness between the United States and Bonaparte's France. His themes are those which will pervade his lifetime of work: the importance of the constitutional Union, the need for each generation to think about preceding and succeeding ones, and the su-

45

premacy of the United States. Much more interesting about this speech are Webster's motifs—the words, images, and other tropes that give form to his issues and themes.

Webster opened his first civic address with language stressing the unity of his audience and, by extension, of his countrymen. "Countrymen, Brethren, and Fathers," he began, "we are now assembled to celebrate an anniversary, ever to be held in dear remembrance by the the sons of freedom."[9] After greeting young and old and pledging that his generation shared their parents' love of freedom, Webster defined his topic and approach for the day:

> On occasions like this, you have heretofore been addressed, from this stage, on the nature, the origin, the expediency of civil government. The field of political speculation has here been explored, by persons, possessing talents, to which the speaker of the day can have no pretensions. Declining therefore a dissertation on the principles of civil polity, you will indulge me in slightly sketching on those events, which have originated, nurtured, and raised to its present grandeur the empire of Columbia (vol. 15, p. 476).

Rather than give a technical explanation of American government, Webster chose to speak of its history—and to do so not by a strictly factual account, but by *sketching* events and episodes. He divided the history of the United States into chapters or sections, presenting them as if they were so many scenes in a diorama. First came the colonial settlement (with predictable concentration on New England): "We behold a feeble band of colonists," he told his audience as he drew them into his fictive spell with the present indicative. (Vol. 15, p. 476). He pictured their plight with lively words: "Destitute of convenient habitations, the inclemencies of the seasons attacked them, the midnight beasts of prey prowled terribly around them, and the more portentious yell of savage fury incessantly assailed them." (vol. 15, p. 476). All the complexities of colonization Webster reduced to these simple moving images. Turning to the events leading up to the Declaration of Independence, Webster spoke in words that showed how he thought of himself as an illustrator. "We might now *display* the Legislatures of the several States . . ." he said; and "On the other hand, we could *exhibit* a British Parliament . . . [or] we could *show* our brethren attacked and slaughtered at Lexington." (vol. 15, p. 477). Displaying, exhibiting, and showing these moments even as he ostensibly passed them over, Webster moved swiftly to the first Independence Day. Once again, he chose to translate the mundane even if highly significant details of that day into a powerful image. "The 4th day of July is now arrived," he told his listeners, "and America, manfully springing from the torturing fangs of the British Lion, now rises majestic in the pride of her sovereignty, and bids her Eagle elevate his wings." (vol. 15, p. 478). Notice the change of tense: most of the speech's descriptions are cast in the past tense, but to achieve special dramatic effect, and to once again make his audience part of the story he was telling by the use of "ideal presence," Webster switched at key moments to the present tense. "The great drama is now completed," he proclaimed, "our Independence is now acknowledged and the hopes of our enemies are now blasted forever. Columbia is now seated in the forum of nations, and the empires of the world are lost in the bright elegance of her glory." (vol. 15, p. 479). He conflated the past and present with his hopes for the future (since in 1800 the USA had not quite achieved all that Webster described) and merged fiction with history.

Having made the Hanoverians witnesses to recreated history, Webster praised the constitutional Union and imagined a glorious future for the country, then paused "to drop the tear of affection over the graves of our departed warriors." (vol. 15, p. 481). To a degree, what follows is a fairly common trope—a catalog of dead heroes including Wooster, Montgomery, Mercer, Greene, and others. More interesting is what Webster had to say about the ultimate hero, the character who would appear in scores of his speeches for the decades to come. "With hearts penetrated by unutterable grief," he said, "we are at length constrained to ask, where is our Washington . . . who came upon our enemies like the storms of winter; and scattered them like leaves before the Borean blast? Where, O my country! is thy political saviour? where, O humanity? thy favorite son?" (vol. 15, p. 481). Telling his audience that "the dark dominions of the grave long since received him," (vol. 15, p. 482), Webster then portrayed the national mourning, picturing individuals who stood artistically for the very people to whom he spoke. "The hoary headed patriot of '76 still tells the mournful story to the listening infant . . . [t]he aged matron still laments the loss of the man, beneath whose banners her husband has fought . . . [and] the sympathetic tear glistens in the eye of every youthful hero." (vol. 15, p. 482). Webster had more than the obvious sentimental reason for depicting such loyal devotion to Washington and his memory, as his quick praise for the second president makes clear: "We console ourselves," he claimed in transparent partisanship that certainly did not capture the truth of the country on the verge of Jefferson's election, "with the reflection that his virtuous compatriot, his worthy successor, the firm, the wise, the inflexible Adams still survives." (vol. 15, p. 482).

Webster concluded his speech with some jingoistic sabre rattling. Bragging a bit prematurely that Britain "twice humbled for her aggressions, has at length been taught to respect us," he vowed that if France presumed to "dictate terms to sovereign America," the force of American arms would put Bonaparte, "the gasconading pilgrim of Egypt" swiftly in his place. (vol. 15, p. 483). Webster spoke directly to his classmates, calling on them to fulfill their obligation to the fathers who had fought for and won the country's freedom. Since actual combat seemed unlikely in 1800, Webster probably really meant that they should vote Federalist against Jefferson the Democrat-Republican, considered by some a Jacobite, atheist, and disciple of Bonaparte. Webster could have put his message quite effectively in simple and straightforward words, but he chose instead to present the prospect of ideological betrayal in apocalyptic imagery: "Ere the religion we profess, and the privileges we enjoy, are sacrificed at the shrines of despots and demagogues, let the pillars of creation tremble! let world be wrecked on world, and systems rush to ruin!" (vol. 15, p. 484).

Much of Webster's style in this early address is, as Edwin Percy Whipple described it, "blazing with cheap jewelry of rhetoric."[10] The demands of the courtroom and the example of Jeremiah Mason would eventually teach Webster to develop a more economical diction, but the motifs and rhetorical strategies of his collegiate speeches persist throughout his career. With instincts and training for poetic devices, Webster knew full well how much more powerfully he could appeal to the Will than to the Understanding. He explained the value of such techniques for political ends in the great work of myth-history that first brought him national attention, "The First Settlement of New England." "Poetry," he said,

is . . . but the handmaiden of true philosophy and morality; it deals with us as human beings, naturally reverencing those whose visible connection with this state of existence is severed, and who may yet exercise we know not sympathy with ourselves; and when it carries us forward, also, and shows us the long continued result of all the good we do, in the prosperity of those who follow us, till it bears us from ourselves, and absorbs us in an intense interest for what shall happen to the generations after us, it speaks only in the language of our nature, and affects us with sentiments which belong to us as human beings.[11]

Apart from a few comments in letters and occasional digressions like the above in his speeches, Webster rarely commented on the aesthetics that shaped his orations. Two speeches, though, do address this subject directly: his 1809 talk to the Dartmouth Phi Beta Kappa, entitled "The State of Our Literature," and the 1852 address "The Dignity and Importance of History," delivered to the New-York Historical Society. Spanning Webster's career, these two speeches provide key insights into how he approached his role as a communicator of public beliefs and values. And they highlight the importance of how he merged fact and fiction.

The 1809 "The State of Our Literature" fits squarely into the critical pattern of its day. Recently freed from their political masters, the independent citizens of the United States wanted cultural and artistic autonomy as well. Swinging between hope and despair, the writers and critics of the young republic called out for a variety of changes in their literary state—innovations including the adoption of new and specifically American subject matters, better educated readers, and even a protective tariff to foster the country's infant intellectual industry.[12]

Appropriately for a time when the country had so much to accomplish and so many worries that it would fail, Webster premised his talk on the belief that men and women and their society could be improved. "Man," said Webster, ". . . in his mental powers, and in his moral sentiments, is the creature of cultivation."[13] Declaring this principle "the foundation of all literary exertion," Webster revealed his utilitarian view of belles-lettres even as he regretted how poorly trained his countrymen were. He believed that Americans had the necessary talent; their literary instincts he traced back to the nation's very founding. "Her first colonists were scholars," he claimed. ". . . [America] is the plantation of enlightened men, from the best informed nations of Europe, in a new country, who were anxious to strew the seeds of knowledge at the birth and beginning of their Republic." (vol. 15, p. 578). Northern colonists in particular "disseminated the elements of knowledge more generally than hath been done at any other time or place." (vol. 15, p. 576).

Despite the country's auspicious beginnings, Webster thought that America had failed to fulfill its artistic promise. Poetry "appeared . . . nowhere but in the corner of a newsprint" and "the terms and language of [painting and sculpture] are unknown even in our best schools." (vol. 15, p. 577). Society had neglected its cultural duty, leaving literature to waste away without the proper attention. Like many others who criticized American culture, Webster blamed "the ruling passion of the country"—worldly ambition. He rejected the common arguments that America lacked sufficient antiquity to produce great writers or that the New World offered no fit subject matters. Webster left Americans no excuses:

The deficiency is ascribable to nothing but the poverty of literary spirit. Like the barbarian who treads, heedless of their value, on the pearl and the topaz which the ocean washes to his feet, we slumber on the best means of scientific improvement ignorant of their worth. A want of literary spirit is followed by a dearth of literary production. (vol. 15, pp. 576–577).

Webster proposed a system of patronage to solve the problem. "Genius will not display itself unpatronized, and unregarded," he explained, "It is coy and will be wooed; it is proud and will be soothed." (vol. 15, p. 577). These words must have heartened any aspiring poets and dramatists in Webster's audience, but he had in mind a much more obviously useful type of writing—history. He proposed the establishment of historical societies, "one of the most easy, and most useful associations of literary men . . . an object of primary consideration, in every country that is desirous of giving its history to posterity." (vol. 15, p. 577). Webster also encouraged governmental support for colleges and universities. "Am I heard by legislators?" he asked; "I would say, as you value your country's glory or your own fame, rear high the fabric of national knowledge." (vol. 15, p. 579). This program of public education and public collection of materials comprised an overall public aesthetic quite in keeping with republican ideals. Through their institutions, Americans would provide their own cultivation and patronage and would write about themselves: patron, author, and subject all together.

While suggesting that such historical writing might lead eventually to more belletristic writing, Webster stressed the immediate practical aspects of American histories. "The duty of the American Scholar," he insisted,

grows out of the circumstances of his country. . . . To warm the apathy, to subdue the avarice, to soften the political asperity of the nation are the objects for the prosecution of which every man of letters stands pledged to the cause he hath espoused. The undertaking tho' arduous, is not hopeless. Every motive of duty and patriotism comprises to invigorate the mind in the pursuit. Let science assume its proper character and discharge its incumbent duties. Let it trample on the paltry distinctions with which little men make themselves known. Let it tread party and passion beneath its feet. And let its earliest, and latest, acquisitions, the blossom and the fruit, be consecrated to the service of our country, and the benefit of mankind. (vol. 15, p. 582).

Perhaps with an eye to his own future, Webster urged young men of political ambition to immerse themselves in history. "The champion of a political party appears, and struts his little hour upon the stage, and straight is heard no more," (vol. 15, p. 580), he warned in words that showed his own familiarity with literature. "Let the emulous youth who pants for renown, think and act for posterity, for posterity will appreciate the obligation. Disregarding momentary considerations, let him build on a lasting foundation." (vol. 15, p. 581).

52

All this talk of scholarship rising above partisan squabbles may have sounded noble and sincere, but spoken by Daniel Webster, it hardly sprang from non-partisan motives. As we noted in looking at his 1800 speech to Hanover, Webster had a strong commitment to the Federalists. In 1809, the year he gave the Phi Beta Kappa address at hand, Webster was a leader of the Young Federalists in Portsmouth. With his loyalties so deeply held—and his party in danger of extinction—Webster had a particular bias when he spoke of historical writing as necessary for cultural survival.

Webster wanted to view and to portray the past in narrative terms that would make his ideals and party, not those of Jefferson and Madison, the logical themes and heroes of America's story. We saw that in the 1800 speech, and we find it as well in Webster's most important address from this period, the 1812 "Address before the Washington Benevolent Society," delivered on Independence Day in Portsmouth. Speaking in the pose of an historian, Webster began by inviting his listeners to contemplate the past. "It is in the power of every generation," he said, "to make themselves, in some degree partakers in the deeds, and in the fame of their ancestors, by adopting their principles, and studying their examples." He continued in words reminiscent perhaps of Edmund Burke:

Wherever history records the acts of men, the past has more or less influence on the present. The heart, as well as the understanding, feels the connection. There is not only a transmission of ideas and knowledge, from generation to generation; there is a traditional communication of sentiments and feelings. The mind delights to associate with the spirits that have gone before it; to enter into their counsels; to embrace their designs; to feel the impulse of their motives; to enjoy their triumphs, and to hold common sorrow in their misfortunes. It exults to find itself, not a distinct, confined point of present being, without relation to the past, or future, but a part of the great chain of existence, which commencing with the origin of our race, and running through its successive generations, binding the present to the past, and even to the future, in mutual attachments, sympathies and common desires [which] hold on to the period, when all sentiments and all affections merely human shall be no more.[14]

History serves humanity, in other words, by guiding the present and the future. Whoever controls the history will influence as well the actions of his or her countrymen. As we would imagine, Webster used his Portsmouth address to attack the Democrat-Republicans in many regards, and he did so by telling his own version of American history and of the life of George Washington. Caring not a whit for the clear facts and cold details of Washington's Administration, Webster turned him into a character. (See Chapter Three for a discussion of Webster's use of Washington in this speech.)

Along with "The State of Our Literature," Webster made one other lengthy public pronouncement on his aesthetic of history, the 1852 "The Dignity and Importance of History" that he delivered to the New-York Historical Society. Just as the 1809 speech looked forward to how Webster would treat historical subjects, so does this speech look back on a career of talking about America. Despite the decades between them, the two speeches resemble each other remarkably.

In 1809 Webster called for the establishment of depositories to collect records and documents. In 1852 he referred to those very institutions as merely "auxiliary to historical composition."[15] Appreciating that they "collect the materials from which the great narrative of events is, in due time to be framed" (vol. 13, p. 463), Webster nonetheless saw important limits on the same societies that he had helped found. "But these collections are not history," he said, "they are only elements of history. History is a higher name, and imports literary productions of the first order." (vol. 13, p. 463). Webster considered this higher order of history a class of belles-lettres:

Well written history must always be the result of genius and taste, as well as of research and study. It stands next to epic poetry, among the productions of the human mind. . . . The province of the epic is the poetical narrative of real or supposed events, and the representation of real, or at least natural, characters; and history, in its noblest examples, is an account of occurrences in which great events are commemorated, and distinguished men appear as agents and actors. (vol. 13, pp. 463-464).

Webster believed that historians had to rely on facts, but he still believed them writers of "a higher order," more poets than annalists. "It is not far from truth to say," he explained, "that well written and classic history is the epic of real life." (vol. 13, pp. 464–465).

How sharply did Webster draw his line between epic and history? On the one hand he argued that history, "while it illustrates and adorns, confines itself to facts, and to the relation of actual events," but on the other he insisted that history had to place "the actions of men in an attractive and interesting light." (vol. 13, pp. 464–465). Considering history as a literary form, Webster had in mind something quite different from factual documentary accounts and analysis:

The first element of history, therefore, is truthfulness; and this truthfulness must be displayed in a concrete form. Classical history is not a memoir. It is not a crude collection of acts, occurrences, and dates. It adopts nothing that is not true; but it does not embrace all minor truths and all minor transactions. It is a composition, a production, which has unity of design, like a work of statuary or of painting. Its parts, therefore, are to be properly adjusted and well proportioned. The historian is an artist, as true to facts as other artists are to nature, and though he may sometimes embellish, he never misrepresents; he may occasionally, perhaps, color too highly, but the truth is still visible through the lights and shades. This unity of design seems essential to all great productions. (vol. 13, p. 465).

This key passage may seem self-contradictory if we confuse *factuality* with *truthfulness*. The former exists in "acts, observances, and dates"; the latter has a less tangible (and less readily tested) quality. Truthfulness represents the meaning or significance of a work, the theme that the unified design serves. As Webster explained, "The best historical productions of ancient and modern times have been written with equal fidelity to one leading thought or purpose." (vol. 13, p. 465). True to the principles of his 1809 address, Webster considered history a utilitarian genre and worried that too much factual detail could actually blunt its edge. "[T]he example of the past, before it can become a useful instructor to the present," he explained, "must be reduced to the elementary principles in human nature, freed from the influence of conditions which were temporary and have changed. . . ." (vol. 13, pp. 466–467). Webster added, "[H]istorical facts are to be related with rather a close and exclusive regard to such and such only as are important." (vol. 13, p. 480). He not only allowed for the artistic touch in history; he demanded it, refusing to allow mere facts to cloud the poetic vision of "the epic of real life."

Having merged history with epic even as he claimed to separate them, Webster spent the next portion of his speech discussing various historians and poets. He spoke almost in the same breath of the "historians" Sallust and Thucydides, and the "artists" Chaucer, Spenser, Milton, and Gray. Webster saw history as a child—rather than a cousin—of imaginative poetry. In his remarks on these writers and their work, Webster noted the ability to select and deploy facts in support of overarching themes. He criticized Livy for including too much information, and praised Sallust—a politician and ally of Caesar whose writings are biased to the verge of being out-and-out propaganda—for taking care "only that there shall be one, deep, clear, strong, and rapid current, to convey him and his thoughts to their destined end." (vol. 13, p. 478). And, Webster might have added, to sweep the reader along as well.

As students of nineteenth-century historiography will recognize, Webster was not saying anything unique.[16] Whether or not Webster was an original thinker on this matter makes no difference, though. What matters is that he believed what he did while in a position of great authority. Even after a certain loss of stature in 1850, Webster remained one of the most potent voices in America. Many people believed in what Webster said about America's past and potential future—and they evidently did so without thinking about the overtly artificial and propagandistic nature of his myth-histories. Evidence abounded for their consideration: Webster's audience at the New-York Historical Society had to search no farther than the very speech they heard that night to find an instance of epic history that deserved more careful scrutiny. Webster devoted the last part of his speech to his own highly crafted version of American history. "Gentlemen," he announced in a sudden transition from his discussion of historians and poets, "I must not dwell upon these general topics. We are Americans . . . and it may well become us to reflect on the topics and means furnished for historical composition in our own land." (vol. 13, p. 483).

Webster began by dividing America's past into three epochs: from 1620 to the First Continental Congress in 1774; from 1774 to the establishment of the Federal government under the Constitution in 1789; and from 1789 to 1852 and beyond. With an eye to his political theme, though, he immediately discarded the very scheme that he had just outlined, preferring instead to consider the third period as running from 1774 to the end of Washington's Administration in 1796. Webster claimed that using this division he could avoid touching on recent controversies. Actually, by concentrating on the period that he chose and characterizing it as the season of the Union's birth, Webster could address the pressing issues of 1852 more effectively by indirection and historical analogy than he could by facing them squarely. Webster's discourse exemplifies his myth of the constitutional Union; it is not a fair account of history, but a thinly disguised device to support the Compromise Measures of 1850 and to quash sectionalism.

Between 1774 and 1796, America achieved independence and established the Union. Webster skipped quickly over the first of these accomplishments, perhaps because rebellion and civil independence had frightening significance in 1852. He made national unity his grand theme, his "one, deep, clear, strong and rapid current." He began with 1774 not because of its revolutionary importance, but for its meaning in Unionist terms: "to trace the events and occurrences which showed the necessity of a general government . . . and which prepared the minds of the people for the adoption of the present Constitution." (vol. 13, p. 484). "No doubt," said Webster, "the assembly of the first Continental Congress may be regarded as the era at which the union of the States commenced." (vol. 13, p. 484).

Each episode of Webster's history of the United States contributes to his overall design. Three scenes illustrate his presentation of the past in simplified narrative terms by using detail and circumstance with exactly the editorial eye that he had just prescribed. Omitting the many quarrels between delegates at the 1774 Congress, Webster drew a scene that he could offer as a model for his contemporaries in 1852:

Let this day [i.e., September 5, 1774] be ever remembered! It saw assembled from the several Colonies those great men whose names have come down to us, and will descend to all posterity. . . . At that day, probably, there could have been convened on no part of this globe an equal number of men, possessing greater talents and ability, or animated by a higher and more patriotic motive. They were men full of the spirit of the occasion, imbued deeply with the general sentiment of the country, of large comprehension, of long foresight, and of few words. . . . They knew the history of the past, they were alive to the difficulties and all the duties of the present, and they acted from the first, as if the future were all open before them. (vol. 13, p. 485).

In case anyone were to miss his point, Webster told his audience exactly how they should perceive this convocation. "Its members," he said, "should be regarded not only individually, but as in a group." (vol. 13, p. 490). He meant this description to show his own generation how to act during the crisis of the 1850s: unified with a full awareness of their national significance and looking to the past for the inspiration of the future.

Webster also pictured the inauguration of George Washington with the same didactic intentions. "I see ten thousand faces anxious to look on him to whose wisdom, prudence, and patriotism the destinies of the country are now committed," he imagined:

I see the august form, I behold the serene face of Washington; I observe his reverent manner when he rises in the presence of countless multitudes, and, looking up with religious awe to heaven, solemnly swears before those multitudes and before Him that sitteth on the circle of those heavens, that he will support the Constitution of his country, so help him God! (vol. 13, p. 487).

Webster's rhetorical Washington swore to do precisely what Webster himself was working so hard to persuade his countrymen to do in 1852. Of course, others who opposed Webster often cited Washington as a champion of nullification and secession.

Webster's third scene depicted the Constitutional Convention, the central moment in his vision of a unified country. By juxtaposing this scene with classical histories, Webster again stressed its quality as part of a new historic dispensation: "Neither Thucydides nor Xenophon, neither Sallust nor Livy, presents any picture of an assembly of public men, or any scene of history which, in its proper grandeur, or its large and lasting influence upon the happiness of mankind, equals this." (vol. 13, p. 491). All three of these pictures from Webster's historical pageant (which is what his account most resembles, a collection of moments presented purely for instantaneous effect, even without regard for chronological order) reveal how he viewed the past with an artist's eye. The First Continental Congress he called "an illustrious *chapter* in our American history." (vol. 13, p. 490). Recounting the inauguration, he said, "I bring the whole *scene* with all its deep interests, before me." (vol. 13, p. 490). And he called his vision of the Constitutional Convention a *"picture"* (vol. 13, p. 491), grander than any made by the ancient historians whom he had praised as "our great teachers and examples in the historical *art*." (vol. 13, p. 473). "I love to travel back in imagination," he said, recalling to us Kames' "waking dream" of ideal presence, "to place myself in the midst of . . . this Union of greatness and patriotism." (vol. 13, p. 490).

Within the narrative context of this epic, Webster turned in his closing words to the circumstances of 1852. He compared the crisis of that time to what the First Continental Congress encountered, calling for his contemporaries to behave in the way that he said their forefathers had. The men of 1774 had acted with an awareness of their place in history—or of their role in the great plot—and his generation of Americans had to follow their example. If Americans would "maintain those institutions of government and that political union," he told the listeners for whom he had just crafted his story of unity and harmony,

We may be sure of one thing, that while our country affords materials for a thousand masters of the historic art, it will afford no topic for a Gibbon. It will have no decline and fall. It will go on prospering and to prosper. . . . Should that catastrophe happen, let it have no history! Let its fate be like that of the lost books of Livy, which no human eye shall ever read, or the missing Pleiad, of which no man can ever know more than that it is lost, and lost forever! (vol. 13, pp. 492–493).

Conspicuously absent from the address until this point, Gibbon's history of Rome loomed in the back of Webster's vision of America. As if realizing how easily life could imitate art, and fearing perhaps that to grant even the imagined possibility of disunion could threaten his country, Webster made it an aesthetic impossibility: such a scene simply would not fit the *truthfulness* of his narrative.

Webster's brief vision of America illustrates perfectly his aesthetic of history. Drawing selectively from the records of the period under consideration, he composed a history entirely for the use of the present, not to illuminate the past with any real respect for its specifics. Leaving out details that might have complicated or detracted from the singularity of his theme, Webster made facts subordinate to theme, translating episodes into a deliberate plot. His wise heroes were not individuals with diverse personalities and political agendas, but allegorical types for his own ideas.

By a happy coincidence, Webster spoke to the Historical Society on February 23, the day following George Washington's birthday. He centered his peroration on this anniversary—even though to make the holiday fit the speech he had to brutalize the calendar somewhat. "It is the anniversary of the birth of Washington," he proclaimed with slight inaccuracy for the sake of truthfulness,

we should know this even if we had lost our calendars, for we should be reminded of it by the shouts of joy and gladness. The whole atmosphere is redolent of his name; hills and forests, rocks and rivers, echo and re-echo his praises. All the good whether learned or unlearned, high or low, rich or poor feel this day that there is one treasure common to them all, and that is the fame and character of Washington. They recount his deeds, ponder over his principles and teachings, and resolve to be more and more guided by them in the future. (vol. 13, p. 496).

Americans celebrated Washington's birthday, in other words, by *studying history*—but history only as conceived and interpreted by Webster. Turning from the past to the present, Webster made his contemporaries characters in his larger narrative of American destiny, and they fulfilled their part chiefly by studying their own story as he wrote it: reader, narrator, and characters merged.

3. Epics of Real Life

To bolster his vision of America's character and meaning, Webster created a mythic past for the country's guidance. He offered the deeds and personalities of his forefathers as guideposts and touchstones for his contemporaries. His studies and work in law and government gave him a broad knowledge of American history; his expertise covered details as well as general trends. He hoped to write documentary histories, but never accomplished this goal.[1] Speaking to large audiences, however, Webster rewrote the past into simple and poetically splendid tales embodying a thematic *truthfulness* for his countrymen. The most important of these myths featured the Pilgrims and the Founding Fathers as the spiritual and political fathers of the Union.

Throughout his career Daniel Webster used the Pilgrims as rhetorical characters serving immediate needs. He delivered three addresses on Pilgrim holidays: "The First Settlement of New England" (1820), "The Landing at Plymouth" (1843), and "The Pilgrim Festival at New York" (1850), and included the Pilgrims in two of his most important speeches on the United States, "The Bunker Hill Monument" (1825) and "The Completion of the Bunker Hill Monument" (1843). The myths that Webster created in these speeches are studies in the exploitation of crafted history and in the speaker's art as a maker of legends.

Webster began "The First Settlement of New England" with a prayer. "Let us rejoice that we behold this day," he said; "Let us be thankful that we have lived to see the bright and happy breaking of the auspicious morn, which commences the third century of the history of New England."[2] Although he came to celebrate New England's past, Webster looked to the future at the very outset by calling the day a commencement rather than a conclusion. The present and future must find their roots in the past.

"Next to the sense of religious duty and moral feeling," Webster argued, "I hardly know what should bear with stronger obligation on a liberal and enlightened mind, than a consciousness of alliance with excellence which is departed; and a consciousness, too, that in its acts and conduct, and even in its sentiments and thoughts, it may be actively operating on the happiness of those who come after it." (vol. 1, pp. 182–183). Establishing America as part of an historic scheme, Webster prepared the philosophical groundwork to support 1620 as a reference for exploring issues of 1820. Loyalty to the past and care for the future were, to his kind, the chief responsibilities for the nation.

"The First Settlement of New England" follows an episodic structure. Its organization is logical, though, and takes its form from Webster's interweaving of past, present, and future. After the introduction, Webster recreated the scene of the first landing, discoursed on America's progress along lines leading to his contemporary concerns, and then turned to

64

the matters of 1820—the nature of Massachusetts government, slavery, and the future of the Union. Webster aimed
at nothing less than the preservation of American society as
he loved it, and in the details of his speech we find his
interpretation of America's past, which he wanted the country
to follow.

Webster depicted the landing and first settlement as the
conquest of elemental strife and wilderness by civilized,
virtuous men and women. Using the first-person point of
view and the present tense, he dramatically presented the
scene as he heightened the moment for his audience and
built a sympathetic identification with the Pilgrims. "We seem
even to behold them," Webster said, "as they struggle with
the elements, and, with, toilsome efforts, gain the shore."
The Pilgrims are virtual personifications of particular qualities:
Carver and Bradford have "mild dignity," Standish a "de-
cisive and soldierlike air." Brewster is "devout," Allerton,
"enterprising." (vol. 1, p. 184). Like the characters in a
medieval morality play, the Pilgrims represent abstractions,
not only for their deeds but, more important, for "the gentle
firmness and thoughtfulness of the whole band; their con-
scious joy for danger escaped; their deep solicitude about
dangers to come; their trust in heaven; their high religious
faith, full of confidence and anticipation." (vol. 1, p. 184).
As allegorical creations, Webster's Pilgrims embody qualities
that relate for the most part to attitudes regarding the future.
Enterprise, solicitude about approaching dangers, faith, confidence, and anticipation: these are the traits of men and
women looking ahead. In an imagined speech by a nameless
settler, Webster cast the history of America's first two cen-
turies as a prophecy. Having already given his listeners heroes
who recalled mythic personifications, Webster then presented
an appropriate theater for their drama:

If God prosper us, we shall here begin a new work which shall last for ages; we shall plant here a new society, in the principles of the fullest liberty and the purest religion; we shall subdue this wilderness which is before us; . . . We shall whiten this coast with the canvas of a prosperous commerce; we shall stud the long and winding shore with a hundred cities. That which we sow in weakness shall be raised in strength. From our sincere, but houseless worship, there shall spring splendid temples to record God's goodness; from the simplicity of our social union, there shall arise wise and politic constitutions of government, full of the liberty which we ourselves bring and breathe. (vol. 1, pp. 186–187).

By putting his words into the mouth of a Pilgrim father, Webster appropriated the authority that he had already augmented. Hardly the simple vision of a newly landed settler, the passage epitomizes, as well as any other in his work, Daniel Webster's American Dream. The wintry forests become fields and gardens; cities and temples rise with civilization's victory over the wilderness. In the final and most glorious fruition of the voyage, the united government was the sine qua non of this prophecy.

Religious freedom was the first goal of the settlers; "It is certain, that, although many of them were republicans in principle," said Webster, "we have no evidence that our New England ancestors would have emigrated . . . merely from their dislike of the political systems of Europe." (vol. 1, p. 188). Spiritual motives soon gave way to more mundane concerns, though. Webster saw inklings of an independence movement at the very landing at Plymouth:

They came hither to a land from which they were never to return. Hither they had brought, and here they were to fix, their hopes, their attachments, and their objects in life. . . . A new existence awaited them here; and when they saw these shores, rough, cold, barbarous, and barren, as then they were, they beheld their country. . . . The morning that beamed on the first night of their repose saw the Pilgrims already *at home* in their country. (vol. 1, pp. 197–198).

"Under the influence of these causes," said Webster, ". . . there was, from the first, a repugnance to an entire submission to the control of British legislation." (vol. 1, pp. 199–200). Finding motives other than their desire for religious freedom, the Pilgrims and those who came after them started America's political and economic rise. Webster apparently did not appreciate differences between the Pilgrims of 1620 and the Puritans who started arriving a decade later.[3] He portrayed all immigration to Massachusetts as belonging to the same movement, and that movement as one for independence. Tracing the progress of the country, Webster converted religious zeal into political rebellion. He praised all early New Englanders as "fit to associate with the boldest asserters of civil liberty" and said that their "firmness of spirit in resisting kingly encroachments in matters of religion, entitled them to the gratitude of their own and succeeding ages." (vol. 1, p. 205). Webster saw a straight line of political descent from the Pilgrim-Puritan first settlers to the Revolutionary generation. Webster stressed the civic deeds of the settlers not only because he believed in this vision of history, but also because he planned to use them to discuss political questions of 1820—the Massachusetts Constitution, slavery, and the Union. Only the second and third of these matters concern us here.

Webster had come out against the admission of Missouri as a slave state in 1820, but he was far from a leader of antislavery forces.[4] He spoke passionately against slavery at Plymouth, basing his attack on New England's Pilgrim heritage. "In the line of conveyance" from the Pilgrims to the future, Webster's generation was duty-bound to preserve the moral and civil standards that their forefathers had set. Having congratulated the country for its many spiritual and tangible successes, Webster reminded New England that all was not right in the world, and that the heirs of the Pilgrims had a special duty in 1820. "As far as experience may show errors in our establishments," said Webster, in language reminiscent of the Puritan jeremiads and of abolitionist speeches and tracts, "we are bound to correct them; and if any practices exist contrary to the principles of justice and humanity within the reach of our laws or our influence, we are inexcusable if we do not exert ourselves to restrain or abolish them." (vol. 1, p. 221). Webster had talked of heroes who reclaimed a barbarous wilderness in the name of Christianity and civilization; transplanted and nourished by the Pilgrims and Revolutionaries, the battle for freedom had won great victories in the New World. Yet, warned Webster, "At the moment when God in his mercy has blessed the Christian world with a universal peace, there is reason to fear, that, to the disgrace of the Christian name and character," (vol. 1, p. 221), slavery and the slave trade threatened to expand. Webster condemned slavery and its business as contrary to the will of God and the course of history and especially repugnant to the heirs of the Pilgrims. He proclaimed:

If there be, within the extent of our knowledge or influence, any participation in this traffic, let us pledge ourselves here, upon the rock of Plymouth, to extirpate and destroy it. It is not fit that the land of the Pilgrims should bear the same any longer. I hear the sound of the hammer, I see the smoke of the furnaces where manacles and fetters are still forged for human limbs. I see the visages of those who work by stealth and at midnight labor in this work of hell, foul and dark, as may become the artificers of such instruments of misery and torture. Let that spot be purified, or let it cease to be of New England. Let it be purified, or let it be set aside from the Christian world; let it be put out of the circle of human sympathies and human regards, and let civilized man henceforth have no communion with it. (vol. 1, p. 221–222).

This was Webster's strongest antislavery statement. When New Englanders accused him of betraying his true ideals by supporting the Compromise of 1850, it was this passage that they had in mind. Webster was actually very careful in 1820 to limit his explicit points to slave trade and New England. He did not call for abolition in Southern states. Although he opposed the Missouri Compromise to some extent, Webster pulled his rhetorical punch to preserve the Union. Having called for his listeners to halt the slave trade "within the extent of our knowledge or *influence*," Webster immediately recalled to them their duty to the Union:

We are bound, not only to maintain the general principles of public liberty, but to support also the existing forms of government which have so well secured its enjoyment, and so highly promoted the public prosperity. It is now more than thirty years that these States have been united under the Federal Constitution, and whatever fortune may await them hereafter, it is impossible that this period should not be regarded as distinguished by signal prosperity and success. (vol. 1, p. 223).

Webster made his priorities clear: slavery was an evil, but the preservation of the Federal Union took precedence over abolition.

"The First Settlement of New England" spoke to the section more than it did to the nation as a whole. Nevertheless, Webster was well on his way to becoming the Defender of the Union in 1820. Having created mythic founders of New England, he used them for his greater national task. The Pilgrims changed in Webster's oratory, turning into increasingly political rather than religious figures, national rather than sectional in their appeal.

Celebrating the glory and success of the Union, "The Bunker Hill Monument" presented America as part of an historical evolution begun in Greece and leading to a world of free republics. The story of western civilization as Webster told it was a movement away from blind and deductive religious, intellectual, and political faith to more decentralized and inductive approaches to these matters. Starting with the Reformation, men increasingly came to depend on their own resources and intelligence to rule their world. The Pilgrims represented a crucial stage in this development; they brought civil freedom within a grand arena and set the course for the Revolutionary and later generations.

As befitted a speech memorializing the American War of Independence, Webster paid only slight attention to the Pilgrims in his first Bunker Hill speech. He limited remarks to only a single paragraph and scattered references—but what he did say continued the pattern in "The First Settlement of New England":

We cherish every memorial of these worthy ancestors; we celebrate their patience and fortitude; we admire their daring enterprise; we teach our children to venerate their piety; and we are justly proud of being descended from men who have set the world an example of founding civil institutions on the great and united principles of human freedom and human knowledge. . . . We shall not stand unmoved on the shore of Plymouth, while the sea continues to wash it; nor will our brethren in another early and ancient Colony forget the place of its first establishment, till their river cease to flow by it.[5]

As he did in the opening of "The First Settlement of New England," Webster stressed virtues necessary to men and women looking to the future. Again he deemphasized the Pilgrims' religion (children must *venerate* but not specifically *imitate* their piety) and portrayed them as political radicals. The new Christian society became an example of civil organization. He significantly linked New England to the South, making Pilgrims and Maryland colonists common ancestors of the nation to come. He turned then quickly to the Revolution and to his overarching object, "OUR COUNTRY, OUR WHOLE COUNTRY, AND NOTHING BUT OUR COUNTRY." (vol. 1, p. 254). Nevertheless, the qualities of the first settlers run through America's history according to Daniel Webster. Enterprise and political freedom were the legacies of the Pilgrims that led to national independence and prepared the way for the Union.

Webster continued in 1843 to manipulate the Pilgrim myth in "The Completion of the Bunker Hill Monument." The Union was in serious trouble over the prospect of annexing Texas and other Mexican territory. Webster feared such expansion not only because it could spread slavery, but also because the debate that it would surely bring could lead to civil war. While in 1825 Webster was optimistic about the Union's future, he was in 1843 profoundly worried.

Looking to the past for hope, Webster created a vision of America's mission that he traced back to the Reformation. "The religious controversies of this period changed society," he said, ". . . they changed man himself."[6] This change inspired migration to the New World:

The spirit of commercial and foreign adventure, therefore, on the one hand, which had gained so much strength and influence since the time of the discovery of America, and, on the other, the assertion and maintenance of religious liberty . . . drawing after it or bringing along with it, as it always does, an ardent devotion to the principle of civil liberty also, were the powerful influences under which character was formed and men trained, for the great work of introducing English civilization, English law, and what is more than all, Anglo Saxon blood, into the wilderness of North America. (vol. 1, p. 271).

Webster stressed not the distinctions between the commercial and religious colonizations that settled the South and North, but rather their connections. Both fired by the political and spiritual aspects of the Reformation, these two movements shared a common English ancestry. North and South in 1843, Webster argued, had a national *character* forged by their past, a cultural mission, and even a blood relationship. Webster referred occasionally to the "Anglo Saxon race" in his late speeches, borrowing the language of Manifest Destiny not to justify expansion but to pull the dissident sons together in their common undertaking. He explicated this Romantic nationalism—a sentimental patriotism that may recall for us

Sir Walter Scott or Frederich von Schlegel—for his Bunker Hill audience. Dismissing the initial differences between colonies as "only enough to create a pleasing variety in the midst of a general family resemblance," he spoke of unity, not division:

> [These differences] disappeared by the progress of time, and the influence of intercourse. The necessity of some degree of Union and cooperation to defend themselves against the savage tribes, tended to excite in them mutual respect and regard. They fought together in the wars against France. The great and common cause of the revolution bound them to one another by new links of brotherhood; and at length the present constitution of government united them happily and gloriously, to form the great republic of the world, and bound up their interests and fortunes, till the whole earth sees that there is now for them, in present possession as well as in future hope, but "One Country, One Constitution, and One Destiny." (vol. 1, p. 271).

"The Landing at Plymouth," also delivered in 1843, followed the same nationalistic theme. Speaking to New York merchants on the anniversary of the first landing, Webster again neglected sectional distinctions for the sake of national cohesion. He made his Pilgrims into only one of several groups of settlers:

> I see today, and we all see, that the descendants of the Puritans who settled upon the Rock of Plymouth; the followers of Raleigh who settled Virginia and North Carolina; he who lives where the truncheon of empire, so to speak, was borne by Smith; the inhabitants of Georgia; he who settled under the auspices of France at the mouth of the Mississippi; the Swede on the Delaware, the Quaker of Pennsylvania,—all find, at this day, their common interest, their common protection, their common *glory*, under the united government. . . ."[7]

Notice how careful Webster was to mention southern colonists.

The last Pilgrim speech, "Pilgrim Festival at New York," belongs to his struggle on behalf of the Compromise of 1850. It is an especially striking example of his Pilgrim myth, because in it Webster both presented a new aspect of his history and ultimately undid his own literary history. Having used the story of the Pilgrims for the Union before, Webster naturally turned to it again in 1850. Yet the story of the first New England settlers had limitations for the present matter; its appeal was primarily sectional. More importantly, Webster's foes had appropriated the Pilgrim myth for their own ends. After decades of prominence, Webster found himself fighting for his role as New England's favorite son and as the interpreter of the region's (and the country's) history and mission. Abolitionists drew their strongest arguments from religion and public morality, combining these appeals with historic precedent and the emotional ties of sectionalism. They used, in other words, the very techniques that Webster had employed with reference to the Pilgrims. Reducing the question to a debate over the things renderable unto Caesar or God, antislavery speakers portrayed the Pilgrims as rebellious forefathers who followed their consciences and not the dictates of the King. In an especially powerful speech that typified the abolitionist rhetoric of the entire decade, Wendell Phillips spoke on December 22, 1855—the anniversary of the first landing—to a Boston audience:

Do you suppose that if Elder Brewster could come up from his grave today, he would be contented with the Congregational Church and the five points of Calvin? No, sir; he would add to his creed the Maine Liquor Law, the Underground Railroad, and the thousand Sharpe's rifles, addressed "Kansas," and labelled "Books."[8]

As his opponents used the Pilgrims against him, Webster must have pondered how rhetorically to recapture the heroic age for the sake of unity and the Compromise. As in 1825 and 1843, he chose to deemphasize the more revolutionary aspects of the Pilgrims as religious dissenters in order to stress their politics. In the earlier speeches, Webster characterized the Pilgrims as civil revolutionaries, but speaking before the Pilgrim Festival he reversed his position completely and spoke of the same political conservatism that he had ignored before.

Toasted by Moses Grinell, President of the New England Society of New York, as the Chief Defender of the Constitution and Union, Webster rose to cheers and opened his speech with an appeal to unity. "Ye sons of New England! Ye brethren of the kindred tie," he began, at once linking his audience with the first settlers. He continued this connection by comparing the weather outside and the political climate of 1850 to the early wretchedness of the colonists:

Gentlemen, this has been a stormy, cold, boistrous, and inclement day. The winds have been harsh, the skies have been severe; and if we had been exposed to their rigor; if we had no shelter against this howling and freezing tempest; if we were wan and worn out; if half of us were sick and tired, and ready to descend into the grave; if we were on the bleak coast of Plymouth, houseless, homeless, with nothing over our heads but the heavens, and that God who sits above the heavens; . . . we should see something, and feel something of that scene, which, in the Providence of God, was enacted at Plymouth on the 22nd of December, 1620.[9]

Webster created here a metaphor for his own time of crisis. He often described the course of American history as a sea voyage; just as the Pilgrims survived storms at sea and found shelter in their new land and homes, so in 1850 did the nation face danger in the debate over slavery. The edifice of the Union provided safety and shelter. Webster made the metaphor explicit later in the speech. Pointing to a confectionary model of The Mayflower, he declared:

Gentlemen, let her be considered this night as an emblem of New England, the New England which now is. New England is a ship, staunch, strong, well built, and particularly well manned. She may be occasionally thrown into the trough of the sea by the violence of winds and waves, she may *wallow* there for a time; but, depend on it, she will right herself. She will ere long *come round to the wind and obey her helm.* (vol. 4, p. 223).

To survive the emergency of 1850, Americans had to follow this example of the Pilgrims: they had to sail straight through the storm to the haven of Union. As he did in 1820 and 1825, Webster tallied Pilgrim virtues—the "stern virtues" of resolution, patience, and religious faith—to assist the country through the danger of the present crisis. Although he praised religion in general terms, Webster could not give it too much authority, since that would have played into the hands of the abolitionists. To rebut their argument that religion required disobedience of civil laws, Webster changed his Pilgrims and, strikingly, finally abandoned them altogether in his rhetoric.

"Gentlemen," he told his audience after praising the Pilgrims, "the scenes of this world change. What our ancestors saw and felt, we shall not see nor feel. What they achieved, it is denied to us even to attempt." This rhetoric seems to echo Webster's earlier insistence that the duty of his generation was preservation and not imitation. He moved beyond his usual attitude, though, and spoke quite specifically about Pilgrim intolerance of other religions. In doing so he reversed his position on the Pilgrims' remarkable liberality expressed in "The First Settlement of New England," rejected their example, and called for more modern and generous cooperation between differing parties. "Their rigid sentiments, and their tenets, apparently harsh and exclusive, we are not called on, in every respect, to imitate or commend." (vol. 4, p. 218). Praising the new tolerant dispensation that he labelled "the American destiny," (vol. 4, p. 219), Webster turned away from the past. Predicting a continent-wide spread of this new liberality, he envisioned a nation in which local interests could live harmoniously.

Webster's mood was one of compromise and conciliation. Loyalty to all Pilgrim virtues had no place in the America of 1850. He certainly could not just dismiss the Pilgrims; his own speeches and the addresses of others forced him to admit their historical relevance. Instead, he transformed his myth of the Pilgrims and refuted abolitionists who argued that the religious quest of the first settlers was the basis of the political rebellion in the colonies:

Religion is both a communication and a tie between man and his Maker; and to his own master every man standeth or falleth. But when men come together in a society, establish social relations, and form governments for the protection of the rights of all, then it is indispensable that this right of private judgement should in some measure be relinquished and made subservient to the judgement of the whole. Religion may exist while every man is left responsible only to God. Society, civil rule, the civil state, cannot exist, while every man is responsible to nobody and to nothing but his own opinion. (vol. 4, p. 220).

While Phillips and his fellows found the Pilgrims models of civil disobedience, Webster in 1850 saw them as men of high morals and steadfast religion who nonetheless realized the necessity of rendering the right things unto Caesar. Exhibiting the legal instincts of a great constitutional lawyer, Webster read aloud the Mayflower Compact (he called it a constitution) and interpreted it as precedent for loyalty and not for rebellion. The Pilgrims might have had religious ends, but Webster preferred the promise of "all due submission and obedience" to the laws, acts, constitutions, and offices of the colony and king. He allowed no debate on the matter: the balance between personal religious belief and civil obligation he called "the very ligament, the very tie, which connects man to man, in a social system." (vol. 4, p. 221). Any doubters could find undeniable evidence of that principle in the example of the Pilgrims and in the United States Constitution. Webster's 1850 account of Plymouth Colony is of a Golden Age marked by conservatism and concord: a model for 1850 and the future.

Webster used a nameless prophet in "The First Settlement of New England" to present the growth of Christianity and civilization into the wilderness. To celebrate America's glorious accomplishments and coming prosperity in 1850, Webster chose William Brewster, the Pilgrim leader whom Phillips would use five years later. Webster's Brewster congratulated his descendants on their civil and commercial success, wished them more of the same, urged that they always cherish the spirit of liberality and cooperation that he claimed marked the first New Englanders, and—almost as if Webster had the counterexample of the abolitionists' Pilgrims in mind—said, "We reproach you not." (vol. 4, p. 222).

Following this benediction, Webster pointed to the sugary *Mayflower* with his promise that New England would soon return to its true course. His vision of America's sublime future recalled the lofty optimism of the twenties:

As for the rest, let us take courage. The day spring from on high has visited us; the country has been called back to conscience and duty. *There is no longer imminent danger of dissolution in these United States.* We shall live as united Americans; and those who supposed they could sever us, that they could rend one American heart from another, and that speculation and hypothesis, that secession and metaphysics, could tear us asunder, will find themselves mistaken. (vol. 4, p. 225).

Perhaps it is our knowledge of what was to come, or maybe it is some repressed hint of anxiety that runs through his rhetoric, that gives Webster's words a hollow, sad ring.

Nothing meant more to Webster than the preservation of the American Union. He abhorred slavery, but chose to tolerate it rather than risk disunion. He loved New England and its particular character and values, yet when sectionalism threatened the Union he put aside the uniqueness of his region and its settlers. At Plymouth in 1820, Webster scorned slavery, but stopped short of rejecting the Missouri Compromise and made an appeal for national unity. As sectional quarrels grew more frightening, he tried to strip the Pilgrim heritage of the moral weight that inspired abolitionists, and spoke instead of the kinship between Northern and Southern colonies and states. Facing in 1850 the greatest challenge of his political life, Webster presented his once revolutionary Pilgrims as mild men who would obey government even if obedience meant defying their religion. This was the sacrifice for which Webster called from the sons of the Pilgrims. Webster himself had helped make the Pilgrim myth part of New England's conscience, but with the Union in danger, Webster transformed his heroes of liberty into models for compromise.

Webster virtually invented the myth of the Pilgrim Fathers, and he used it with great skill and artistry, consciously crafting and recrafting it to suit his needs. But they were only one generation of mythic heroes whom he invoked to support his vision of the Union. Along with the Settlers, Webster spoke often of the Founders—most often of George Washington, who fulfilled the promise of the colonies by creating the Constitution and Union. Washington was Webster's greatest hero. While the Pilgrims figured prominently in only five addresses, Washington appeared in many works all through Webster's long career. Sometimes Webster referred to Washington for detailed precedents regarding fairly unexciting matters. Discussions of British trade in the West Indies, questions about Van Buren's fiscal schemes, and support for the expansion of the navy were all instances in which Webster recalled the policies of the first President. He admired the particular decisions of Washington, and planned to write a three-volume analysis of his Administration.[10]

Webster's citation of Washington the bureaucrat pales next to his loving idolization of Washington the Father of America.

Using the extant Washington myth as the core of his own creation, Webster made a splendidly useful device for a variety of rhetorical ends.[11] In Webster's speeches we find Washington as the only source of political legitimacy, the heroic saint of Federalism and its descendants, the quasi-divine guardian of the Union, and the messiah of a global civil millennium.

Delivered only six months after Washington's death, Webster's 1800 Independence Day address at Hanover was as much a eulogy for Washington as it was a celebration of America's promise. "With hearts penetrated by unutterable grief," said Webster,

we are at length constrained to ask, where is our Washington? where the hero, who led us to victory—where the man, who gave us freedom? Where is he, who headed our feeble army, when destruction threatened us, who came upon our enemies like the storms of winter; and scattered them like leaves before the Borean blast? Where, O my country! is thy political saviour? Where, O humanity! thy favorite son?[12]

Even within these few lines Webster magnified Washington from a man and general to a force of nature and supernature who virtually defeated the English all by himself. The characterization expands: from the leader of an army, Webster's Washington became the political savior of his country and then the favorite son of all humanity. Webster portrayed Washington as a self-sacrificing champion who personified the nation: "The man, who never felt a wound, but when it pierced his country, who never groaned, but when fair freedom bled, is now forever dead." (vol. 15, pp. 481–482).

As he continued the eulogy, Webster spoke not so much about Washington as a dead man as he did about his reincarnation as a national legend:

Though months have rolled away since he left this terrestial orb, and sought the shining worlds on high, yet the sad event is still remembered with increasing sorrow. . . . At the name of Washington, the sympathetic tear still glistens in the eye of every youthful hero, nor does the tender sigh yet cease to heave, in the fair bosom of Columbia's daughters. (vol. 15, p. 482).

The *increasing* memory and sorrow were perhaps not so much honest grief as they were the result of eulogists and politicians who kept Washington's image (adapted, of course, for their specific ends) before the public. John Adams recalled this frenzy in an 1816 letter to Thomas Jefferson. "The Death of Washington," he wrote,

"diffused a general Grief. The old Tories, the Hyper-Federalists, the Speculators sett [sic] up a general Howl—Orations, Prayers, Sermons, Mock Funerals, were all employed, not that they loved Washington, but to keep in Countenance the Funding and Banking Systems; And to cast into the Background and the Shade all others who had been concerned in the Service of their Country in the Revolution."[13]

Webster's 1800 remarks undeniably belong to this tradition: after eulogizing Washington, he praised "his virtuous compatriot, his worthy successor, the firm, the wise, the inflexible Adams," then blasted Jeffersonian measures as treason to Washington.

On July 4, 1802, Webster surveyed the American political scene and found it wanting. Fearing the demise of his party before the rise of democracy, he called for his countrymen to stand by the Constitution and to follow the purest model of patriotism:

There are in all countries a great many monkeys who wish to be thought patriots, and a great many who believe them such. But, because we are often deceived by appearances, let us not believe that the reality does not exist. If our faith is ever shaken, if the crowd of hypocritical demagogues lead us to doubt, we will remember Washington and be convinced; we will cast our eyes around us, on those who have toiled and fought and bled for their country, and we will be persuaded that there is such a thing as real patriotism, and that it is one of the purest and noblest sentiments that can warm the heart of man.[14]

Although less obviously poetic than the 1800 speech, this passage presents Washington in emotional, spiritual terms. Webster's language gives us clues to his method: patriotism he called a pure and noble sentiment that warms the heart— or quickens the soul. Webster described accepting Washington's example (which he would see best manifested by a vote for the Federalists) as a conversion more than merely political. Washington acts in this metaphor as a moral and mystical force inspiring a national regeneration. "Let us cherish true patriotism," said Webster, "in that, there is a sort of inspiration that gives strength and energy almost more than human." (vol. 15, p. 521).

The "Address before the Washington Benevolent Society," one of the most blatantly partisan noncampaign orations Webster gave, epitomized his apotheosis of the first president. "In an hour big with events of not ordinary import," he told his listeners, "we come to take counsel of the dead. . . . We come, to instruct and to fortify our patriotism, by hearkening to the voice, and contemplating the character of him, to whom we owe all that nation ever can owe to mortal achievement."[15] Calling Washington's vision of the country (as Webster interpreted and presented it) "an infallible criterion" for the nation, Webster made a point-by-point comparison of Democrat-Republican policies with precedents set by Washington. Commercial regulation, war with Britain, federal consolidation of power, defense measures—in all these and other matters Webster claimed that his opponents had betrayed the Father of the Country. More than mere political disagreement, this divergence appeared utter blasphemy in Webster's account:

A situation can hardly be imagined more difficult than this nation's in 1793 [when Frenchmen and Americans pressured Washington for war against Britain]. . . . But Washington could neither be intimidated, nor deceived. He saw the path of impartiality and justice open before him.

It was illuminated with all the light of heaven. It conducted to the true glory and happiness of his country. He entered, and pursued it. He triumphed, not only over the designs of foreign nations, but also over the temporary prejudices of a portion of his countrymen. (vol. 15, p. 593).

Washington's eulogists often spoke of him in Biblical terms, comparing him to Joshua, David, and other great leaders. Webster portrayed Washington as a visionary prophet appointed by God to show the True Way to his chosen people. With the light of heaven showing him the path, Washington overthrew his foes with a power not unlike that of Christ in Milton's *Paradise Lost.* In this single passage we find two Washingtons: the cautious politician who handled factions wisely, and the inspired saint who saved his country for divine ends.

Webster made Washington a part of his crusade against nullification. Delivering "The Character of Washington" at a formal dinner in Washington, D. C. on the bicentennial of Washington's birth, he attacked Calhoun by elevating his subject to messianic status and making him the Union's guardian angel. Washington's very name was a source of mystical power in Webster's poetic history, recalling a common religious motif:

That name was of a power to rally a nation. In an hour of thick-thronging public disasters and calamities; that name shone, amid the storm of war, a beacon light, to cheer and guide the country's friends; it flamed, too, like a meteor, to repel her foes. That name, in the days of peace, was a lodestone, attracting to itself a whole people's confidence, a whole people's love, and the whole world's respect. That name, descending with all time, spreading over the whole earth, and uttered in all the languages belonging to the tribes and races of men, will for ever be pronounced with affectionate gratitude by every one in whose breast shall arise an aspiration for human rights and liberty.[16]

Webster invoked not the *example* of Washington as an administrator, but his very name and its talismanic power.

"Washington stands at the head of a new era," proclaimed Webster, "His age and his country are equally full of wonders." (vol. 2, p. 70). Starting with the birth of Washington the world entered into a new dispensation. The spirits of freedom and individuality ushered in a period of progress with Washington leading the way (as he did in the 1812 speech) to the millennium:

By the benignity of Providence, this experiment so full of interest to us and to our posterity for ever, so full of interest, indeed, to the world in its present generation and in all its generations to come, was suffered to commence under the guidance of Washington. Destined for his high career, he was fitted for it by wisdom, by virtue, by patriotism, by discretion, by whatever can inspire confidence in man toward man. (vol. 2, p. 73).

Fired by the holy "spirit of human liberty," (vol. 2, p. 74), Washington served all humanity, and if his work should fail, hope itself would perish. "If this great *Western sun* be struck out of the firmament, at what other fountain shall the lamp of liberty hereafter be lighted?" (vol. 2, p. 74), Webster asked.

Speaking of the virtues of Washington's character and the principles of his administration, Webster told his audience to emulate the first President in both regards. Honesty and selflessness motivated Washington's politics; Webster emphasized nonpartisanship, neutrality toward foreign powers, and domestic accomplishments in finance, defense, and economic growth. These significant achievements Webster ranked below Washington's patronage of the American Union. Turning sub-textually to Calhoun and nullification, Webster ended his catalogue of Washington's virtues with his Unionism. "Finally, Gentlemen, there was in the breast of Washington one sentiment so deeply felt, that no proper occasion escaped without its utterance," he told his companions:

The Union was the great object of his thoughts . . . He regarded the union of these States less as one of our blessings, than as the great treasure-house which contained all of them. Here, in his judgement, was the great magazine of all our means of prosperity; here, as he thought, and as every true American still thinks, are deposited all our animating prospects, all our solid hopes for future greatness (vol. 2, p. 79).

To be truly American, to follow loyally Washington's example—as one had to in Webster's scheme—citizens had to believe in his interpretation of the Constitution. Everything that Washington advised or proscribed affected the Union, which Webster called (using a term from Washington's own "Farewell Address") "the very palladium of their prosperity and safety, and the security of liberty itself." (vol. 2, p. 79).

Webster's Washington was a unique divinely appointed savior. His work was a one-time-only convenant, possible "once in human affairs, and but once." Webster rhetorically dragged his nineteenth-century foes before the god-like Washington. "If we regard our country as personated in the spirit of Washington," he asked:

if we might consider him as representing her, in her past renown, her present prosperity, and her future career, and as in that character demanding of us all to account for our conduct, as political men or as private citizens, how should he answer him who had ventured to talk of disunion and dismemberment? (vol. 2, p. 80).

Washington the Father, the Person of America, would judge the Nullifiers and find them sinful.

So strong was Webster's divine characterization of Washington that his conclusion might imply that Webster had made the President into God: "Let us trust in that Gracious Being who has hitherto held our country as in the hollow of his hand," said Webster; "Let us trust to the influence of Washington's example." (vol. 2, p. 81). The speech ended with a scene of America's future in which united citizens look on "his native mountains . . . the river on whose banks he lived, and on whose banks he rests" (vol. 2, p. 82), protected by the flag of Union. Satanic by implication, John Calhoun and Robert Hayne had no place in the paradise founded by Washington and preserved by Webster and his fellows.

Webster used this apotheosized figure again as part of his work for Clay's Compromise Measures. In his "Speech at Annapolis" he stated his case emphatically and connected it with Washington. Toasted as the "ablest defender" of the Union, Webster began humbly. "Gentlemen," he said, "I am nothing; it is the cause that is everything."[17] Bringing to mind his 1832 remark that he and Washington considered Union the treasure-house of all the riches of the nation, he called the Compromise "the cause upon which depends the maintenance of all the political associations and principles which have made the United States what they are now." (vol. 13, p. 392).

It was a cause, moreover, with the patronage of George Washington. The first President was an especially safe hero in the 1850s, a Southerner of unquestionable nationalism. Webster did not have to neutralize any local associations as he did with the Pilgrims. Citing Washington's letter in support of the Constitution and quoting from his "Farewell Address," Webster stressed his belief in the Union. He pictured Washington as a fatherly spirit watching over and guiding a sometimes errant people who needed reminding of what was best for them:

Gentlemen, Washington with all his sagacity, did not comprehend his own destiny. He did not see the long track of influences which were to follow his revolutionary character. . . . He has never yet performed the work assigned him, and he never will, until the end of time; because, gentlemen, that great and glorious work still subsists, and is going on; he is still upholding, by his precepts, his exhortations, and his example, the importance and the value of this Union of the States. (vol. 13, pp. 393–394).

Together, Washington and his country could survive until *the end of time*. Webster recreated for his Annapolis audience scenes of America's earliest days as a republic, then invoked the ghost of Washington himself. As he did with Elder Brewster in New York, Webster made his hero speak directly to the present:

Nay, I think I hear him say now, in the abodes of the blessed, that, if it were permitted to him, to revisit the earth, and be re-clothed with the bones and the flesh which are mouldering at Mount Vernon, he would appear to his countrymen as when he stood at the head of their armies, or as he appeared to the country in the course of his most glorious administration of this Government, and conjure and adjure them, by every consideration that ought to have weight with men, "Hold on fast by that Constitution which is the only security for the liberty which cost me and my associates seven years of war, of fire, and of blood. (vol. 13, p. 395).

Webster's Washington spoke like a father to his children. Disobedience was antithetical to the American character, impossible by definition: "We are not Americans," said Webster, "if we resist the examples of our predecessors, any more than if we trample upon the Constitution, the work of their hands." (vol. 13, p. 395).

"An Addition to the Capitol," Webster's last Independence Day oration, is striking for the variety of rhetorical techniques with which it supports the Union. The messianic Washington plays an especially important part in the speech. After a long celebration of the Union and a scolding for extremists, Webster took them back in their imaginations to a scene from Washington's life, the original ground-breaking for the Capitol building. He pictured Washington on that day, "dignified and grave," marked by anxiety and concern for the young country.[18] Telling of Washington's progress through the wilderness that became the capitol city, Webster imagined that the first President stood before him in 1850. "Ye men of this generation," said Webster's Washington,

I rejoice and thank God for being able to see that our labors and toils and sacrifices were not in vain. You are prosperous, you are happy, you are grateful; the fire of liberty burns brightly and steadily in your hearts, while DUTY and LAW restrain it from bursting forth in wild and destructive conflagration. Cherish liberty, as you love it; cherish its securities, as you wish to preserve it. Maintain the Constitution which we labored so painfully to establish, and which has been to you such a source of inestimable blessings. Preserve the union of these States, cemented as it was by our prayers, our tears, and our blood. (vol. 13, p. 317).

"Do," in other words, "exactly as Daniel Webster tells you to do." Webster replied to his imagined Washington in the language of a loyal priest to his deity:

Great Father of our Country! we heed your words; we feel their force as if you now uttered them with lips of flesh and blood. Your example teaches us, your affectionate addresses teach us, your public life teaches us, your sense of the value of the blessings of the Union. Those blessings our fathers have tasted, and we have tasted, and still taste. Nor do we intend that those who come after us shall be denied the same high fruition. Our honor as well as our happiness is concerned. We cannot, we dare not, we will not, betray our sacred trust. (vol. 13, p. 317).

So sublime and deified was Webster's characterization of Washington that when he concluded by thanking "the Father of all our mercies, political, social, and religious," (vol. 13, p. 318), his listeners might well have inferred God or that other Father, George Washington.

Webster's Pilgrims and his Washington are the chief examples of how he revised and used historical persons as fictive rhetorical devices. Less problematic than the Pilgrims, Washington stood at the center of Webster's American pantheon. In spite of his adequate knowledge of Washington's foibles and flaws as a man and administrator, Webster presented him as the very soul of all the best about America. "America has furnished to the world the character of Washington," he declared in "The Completion of the Bunker Hill Monument."[19] And for all that the obelisk was a fine symbol of America's power and promise, he preferred the symbol that Washington himself had become:

Towering high above the column which our hands have builded, beheld, not by the inhabitants of a single city or a single State, but by all the families of man, ascends the colossal grandeur of the character and life of Washington. . . . It is the embodiment and vindication of our Transatlantic liberty. . . . [L]iving from infancy to manhood and age amidst our expanding, but not luxurious civilization; partaking in our great destiny of labor, our great contest with unreclaimed nature and uncivilized man, our agony of glory, the war of Independence, our great victory of peace, the formation of the Union, and the establishment of the Constitution; he is all, all our own! . . .

I claim him for America. In all the perils, in every darkened moment of the state, in the midst of the reproaches of enemies and the misgivings of friends, I turn to that transcendent name for courage and for consolation. (vol. 1, pp. 281–282).

Both the son and father of America, Washington towers in Webster's speeches as the watchful guardian angel of the country and as its champion over the world—the hero embodying the promise and virtue of the country and, by virtue of America's role in the world, of God's promise to all humanity.

4. Our Sacred Trust

One of the major questions that historians and biographers face when considering Daniel Webster's characterization of the constitutional Union is his apparent inconsistency. As opponents often noted during his life, Webster's youthful resistance to Federal policies and power in the early years of the century—his furious "Rockingham Memorial" comes to mind—apparently jarred with his later nationalism. We must admit that Webster changed his mind about the legal nature and the intrinsic value of a strong federal government, but he himself denied any significant inconsistency. Attacked as a hypocrite, Webster swore to his dying day that the same principles of unionism underlay all of his politics, no matter how he voted on particular questions. Faced with undeniable differences in Webster's statements on issues in his early and late years, can we find evidence to support his claims? Was there some truth to what he said, or were his protests of innocence merely the stonewalling of a professional politician?

No doubt the cynical explanation has some merit. But we can also find another answer by looking at Webster's dualistic image of the constitutional Union. While Webster's legal vision of the Union did change over the years, its poetic counterpart remained remarkably constant throughout his career. The progress of this bifurcated characterization was not simply from an essentially legal to a mythic idea (or from what Paul Nagel calls experimentalist to absolute)[1], but rather a double movement: Webster's legal construction of the Constitution did change, but the poetic character of his Unionist rhetoric remains remarkably regular throughout his life. We might describe the course of Webster's changing constitutional and unionist rhetoric as the subsumption of his original opinions by his own myth. It was, perhaps, the triumph of artistic truthfulness over factual argument. As he preached with more and more passion to preserve the government united in the face of increasing dangers, Webster reshaped (or even omitted) debatable facts that might be interpreted as contrary to his goal into his overarching myth of the Union—just as he did his portrait of the Pilgrims. At various times in his career, and often within a single speech, we find Webster speaking of the constitutional Union as both a legal arrangement contrived by mortals and as a semidivine entity with a will and a destiny all of its own.

Webster's very first public address, the 1800 Independence Day talk at Hanover, has hints of this double vision. He began that speech by referring to "the iron harvest of the martial field" of the Revolutionary War and rattling a rhetorical saber at Britain and France. He had especially strong words for Napoleon; attacks against the French had a special significance to Americans in 1800, one with domestic as well as foreign implications. The same year, Webster wrote to a friend that enemies abroad, not even Napoleon, were not the real threat. "No, Bingham," he explained, "intestine feuds alone I fear. The French Faction, though quelled, is not eradicated."[2] By "the French Faction," Webster meant Thomas Jefferson and the Democrat-Republicans. When he vowed to his Hanover audience that "the thunder of our cannon shall insure the performance of our treaties, and fulminate destruction of Frenchmen, till old ocean is filled with blood, and gorged with pirates," he was subtextually aiming at the Jeffersonians.[3] Webster made this even more explicit when he suggested the Democrat-Republicans would betray the work of the Founding Fathers. "Our ancestors bravely snatched expiring liberty from the grasp of Britain, whose touch is poison," he said; "shall we now consign it to France, whose embrace is death?" (vol. 15, p. 484).

In the midst of this partisan and jingoistic diatribe, Webster inserted a brief passage on the United States government. Although short and easily overlooked, this digression is central to the speech because it contains the foundations of how Webster spoke of the constitutional Union and—as he saw the situation—of his logical disagreement with the Jeffersonians. The passage deserves quotation in full:

We then [after the Revolution] saw the people of these United States engaged in a transaction, which is, undoubtedly, the greatest approximation towards human perfection the political world ever yet experienced; and which, perhaps, will forever stand in the history of mankind without a parallel. A great Republic, composed of different states, whose interests in all respects could not be perfectly compatible, then came deliberately forward, discarded one system of government and adopted another, without the loss of one man's blood.

There is not a single government now existing in Europe, which is not based on usurpation, and established, if established at all, by the sacrifice of thousands. But in the adoption of the present system of jurisprudence, we see the powers necessary for government voluntarily springing from the people, their only proper origin, and directed to the public good, their only proper object.

With peculiar propriety, we may now felicitate ourselves, on that happy form of mixed government under which we now live. The advantages, resulting to the citizens of the Union, from the operation of the Federal Constitution, are utterly incalculable, and the day, when it was received by a majority of the states, shall stand on the catalogue of American anniversaries second to none but the birthday of Independence. (vol. 15, p. 490).

We find both aspects of Webster's unionism in this passage. The legal view of the Constitution as a human device predominates: the people established the government in a spirit of compromise to improve their economic and political circumstances. Webster called this establishment a transaction, referring to "the adoption of the present system of jurisprudence." This second revolution—the transition from the Articles of the Confederation to the Constitution—was one of laws and conventions that brought the first revolution to fruition. Webster praised the government highly, but only as an *"approximation* towards *human* perfection" in "the *political* world."

On the other hand, Webster attributed a profound moral significance to the Constitution and Union, ascribing to them at least some kind of perfection and suggesting that the Federal government might be immortal and forever unique. Furthermore, though he admitted that the government had been designed with deliberation by human beings who had particular ends in mind, he called the resulting advantages "utterly incalculable." Even while he described the events of 1787–89 in the language of the law, Daniel Webster created the impression of something greater.

Speaking two years later to an audience in Fryeburg, Maine, Webster discussed the Constitution in greater detail. Calling on his listeners "to survey the ground of our national standing; to enquire if the privileges we possess are worth preserving and to reflect on the means requisite for their perpetuation,"[4] Webster used prosaic language. By asking his questions so calmly and by referring to the Constitution and its support as "the means" to perpetuate advantages, he characterized the government as a successful expedient contrived by human beings, but went on to describe it in a different way:

> This instrument is the bond of our union and the charter of our rights. To its operation we are indebted for our national prosperity, happiness and honor. It raised us from a state of anarchy and misrule, reconciled the jarring interests of individual States, and matured the fair fruits of independence. (vol. 15, p. 509).

Even though he referred to the Constitution as an "instrument" and "charter," Webster made it an entity in and of itself. The verbs he used—*reconciled, raised,* and *matured*— show how he changed the legal charter between men into an active principle. His words grew more hyperbolic as he continued:

> It [the Constitution] should be considered as the sacred and inviolable palladium, ready to wither that hand which would lay hold on it with violence. Whatever variety of opinion may exist on other subjects, on this there must be one. Whoever does not wish to perpetuate our present form of Government in its purity, is either weak or wicked; he cannot be the friend of his Country. Whether he wishes to behold America prostrate before a throne or set afloat on the stormy sea of democracy, his principles are equally dangerous and destructive. (vol. 15, p. 509).

Webster left his opponents with no escape. If all questions depended on the Constitution (and only as the Federalist interpreted it), any disagreement became treason. And treason in turn was blasphemy against the *purity* of the *sacred* and *inviolable palladium.* Webster raised the Constitution to something akin to divinity, giving it mystical powers of generation and destruction.

In a second version of the 1802 Fryeburg address, which Webster evidently did not deliver, (vol. 15, p. 509), we find a more striking example of this apotheosis. Celebrating the

Union and Constitution as "blessings of Providence," he warned:

> Beware! If an angel should be winged from Heaven, on an errand of mercy to our country, the first accents that would glow on his lips would be, Beware, be cautious! you have everything to lose; you have nothing to gain. We live under the only government that ever existed which was framed by the unrestrained and deliberate consultations of the people. Miracles do not cluster. (vol. 15, p. 520)

Men may have contrived the United States government, but angels protect it. It is a miracle, a gift from God that has a life and a character all its own, to which the citizens must pay homage.

The years of the Embargo and the War of 1812 increased Webster's sectionalism. Incipient before, this line of argument became more explicit during his first years as an active politician, notably in "Considerations on the Embargo" (1808) and "The Rockingham Memorial" (1812).

George Ticknor Curtis called "Considerations on the Embargo" Webster's entry into politics.[5] If this observation is true, there is no little irony that Webster, the Champion of the Union, should have begun his career with this states'-rightist pamphlet. "The Government of the United States," he wrote in words quite different from his poetic celebrations,

> is a delegated, limited Government. Congress does not possess all the powers of Legislation. The individual States were originally complete sovereignties. They were so many distinct nations, rightfully possessing and exercising, each within its own jurisdiction, all the attributes of supreme power. . . . By the Constitution, they mutually agreed to form a General Government, and to surrender a part of their powers, but not the whole, into the hands of this Government.[6]

"This," he concluded, "is the plain theory of the national Constitution." Preparing to attack the Embargo on the grounds that it exceeded the authority of the Federal government, Webster presented some of the same principles on which

John C. Calhoun would later premise his own doctrine of nullification: fully sovereign at one time, the states retained in some way the right to disagree with and to pass judgment independently on the Federal government.

"Considerations on the Embargo" is strikingly lawyerly in its tone and organization. The "Address Before the Washington Benevolent Society," however, incorporates both Websterian modes. Appropriately for the occasion, Webster framed his opinions by referring to Washington. "It should be our constant aim to exhibit Washington's example as the true fruit and genuine effect of our Revolution," he said; "we should point to his principles of our government, and to his administration as the best practical development and application of these principles."[7] To survive, America had to follow Washington's bureaucratic precedents and accept his legal construction of the Constitution—an interpretation which Webster put in decidedly sectionalist terms in 1812:

The national compact, he saw, guaranteed to the several states not only equal political rights, but also equal protection to their several interests and pursuits. It was designed, not to revolutionize the habits and employments of any section of the country, but to protect the interests of all, in the channels naturally worn for themselves. It was an instrument of preservation, not of change. (vol. 15, p. 586).

Once again, the Constitution is the means to an end ("an instrument"). Watchful for the shipping interests of Portsmouth, Webster spoke for the protection of his own district, and went so far as to insist, "The Federal Constitution was adopted for no single reason so much, as for the protection of commerce." (vol. 15, p. 587). The right to dissent, denied to Democrat-Republicans in the earlier speeches, is the strongest theme of this address.

Webster made his case even more strongly in "The Rockingham Memorial." "We hold the right of judging for ourselves," he wrote about trade restrictions, "and have never yet delegated to any government the power of deciding for us, what pursuits and occupations, best comport with our interests and our situation."[8] The Constitution was designed, he explained, "to protect, by the strong arm of the whole nation, the interests of each particular section." (vol. 15, p. 600). Webster called the actions of the Federal government unconstitutional and inspired by "a fixed and settled resolution in the General Government, to enforce this exhortation by the authority of law, and to accumulate upon us, in the intervals of war, a ponderous, and crushing system of restriction, non-importation, non-intercourse, and embargo." (vol. 15, p. 601). He claimed that the Federal government acted against the values of the Founding Fathers and the Constitution:

> We are, sir, from principle and habit attached to the union of these states, but our attachment is to the substance, and not to the form. It is to the good, which this Union is capable of producing, and not to the evil, which is suffered unnaturally to grow out of it. If the time should arrive, when the Union should be holden together by nothing but the authority of the law, when its incorporating, vital principle shall become extinct . . . when . . . we shall be one not in interest and mutual regard, but in name and form only; we, sir, shall look on that hour, as the closing scene of our country's prosperity. (vol. 15, p. 609).

Webster's prosaic and poetic characterizations of the Union both appear in this passage: the government is at once a legal measure for the benefits of its various partners, and something less earthly: words like substance, good, evil, and vital principle show the real nature of Webster's rejection of a purely legal Union. Without the proper appreciation for the Union as a greater entity, the United States would be meaningless for Webster. He spoke of secession carefully but clearly: "It shall be our most fervent supplication to avert both the event and the occasion, and the Government may be assured, that the tie that binds us to the Union will never be broken, by us." (vol. 15, pp. 609–610). Webster's promise may seem reassuring at first, but to the angry men and women at Rockingham, it was far from a concession to the Federal government. "The tie that binds" refers not to the legal bond of the Constitution, but rather to the mutual love, respect and cooperation of all the states. It means devotion to the Union as Webster described it in extraordinary terms. he had just said so himself; Madison's war threatened to destroy the true Union. So secession became an option that could save the ideal Constitution by sacrificing its legal counterpart. Proclaiming that "no pressure, domestic or foreign" could compel New Hampshire to accept alliance with France, Webster made his position clear:

We have reflected on the measures, which an adherence to this resolution might hereafter occasion. We have considered the events which may grow out of it. In the full and undisguised view of these consequences, we have formed this our resolution, and we affirm to you, sir, and to the world, that it is deep, fixed, and unchangeable. (vol. 15, p. 610)[9]

After the war, with New England finding Federal power less oppressive—and Federal tariffs more useful—Webster became more of a Unionist. It may be that this change had links to his work in the United States Supreme Court. *Dartmouth College* v. *Woodward* (1818), *McCulloch* v. *Maryland* (1819), *Gibbon* v. *Ogden* (1820), and *Ogden* v. *Saunders* (1827) differed in particulars, but they all involved the general question of Federal and state powers.[10] *Dartmouth College* upheld the Federal authority to overrule state legislatures, and provoked Governor Plumer of New Hampshire to call the decision a consolidationist threat to the individual states— exactly the kind of interference that Webster himself had decried in 1812. In his argument for *McCulloch* v. *Maryland,* Webster spoke quite differently from the way he did when avowing that the citizens of New Hampshire had every right to judge Federal laws and act accordingly. Protecting the Bank of the United States from the state of Maryland, Webster held in 1819 that when the people divided authority between their state and national governments, they decreed that the Constitution and the laws passed under it "shall be the supreme laws of the land, and shall control all State legislation and state constitutions, which may be incompatible therewith; and it confides to [the United States Supreme Court] the ultimate power of deciding all questions arising under the Constitution and laws of the United States."[11] The classic expression of Webster's Unionism in these years is "The Second Speech on Foot's Resolution" (1830), better known as "The Second Reply to Hayne." Both prosaically and poetically, this speech was the Unionist centerpiece of the nullification debate. Thinking of the years that Webster had spent arguing for a strong Federal position in the courts, George Ticknor Curtis wrote, "it should . . . be said of Mr. Webster, that he was better fitted than any other man in the Union to encounter in debate the new doctrines that threatened the overthrow of the Constitution."[12] It would seem that Webster's extensive legal knowledge and experience in constitutional debate were his chief assets in this debate, and they were crucial. But Webster's poetic talents were just as important. The technical facets of Webster's argument gave the speech substance, but his imaginative language gave it life.

Webster began by mixing metaphor with an insistence on keeping to the facts. "When the mariner has been tossed for many days in thick weather, and on an unknown sea," he said, "he naturally avails himself of the first pause in the storm, the earliest glance of the sun, to take his latitude, and ascertain how far the elements have driven him off his true course."[13] Having described the debate in these terms, Webster asked that Senator Foot's resolution be read aloud, proclaiming it "almost the only subject about which something has not been said" by Hayne. Webster had justification for this complaint: after Hayne's first criticisms prompted Webster to defend his part of the country, Hayne raised the stakes by attacking New England, the state of Massachusetts, and Webster himself as fair weather patriots. He also offered a formidable analysis of nullification that echoed Webster's own words of 1812. Arguing that the Constitution consolidated the Union but not the government, Hayne drew a distinction similar to that which Webster made years earlier. Only by resisting the usurpation of powers rightfully reserved for the states could the people preserve the true spirit of Union. Curiously, Hayne criticized New England for the Hartford Convention, which had asserted this very principle. That convention, he said, prepared "the way for an open resistance to the government, and a separation of these states."[14] Hayne was considered a first-rate speaker, but his speech on this occasion is marred by self-contradictions, awkward metaphors, and invective. He obviously had two goals: to expound on nullification and, more important, to belittle Webster.

Webster did not take these insults kindly. After deftly ridiculing Hayne (in part by showing how Hayne had misused a Shakespearean allusion that in fact worked against him and not against Webster), Webster defended New England's and his own devotion to the Union. To prove that the North did have the rest of the nation at heart, he spoke first of slavery. Although he opposed it as "one of the greatest evils, both moral and political," Webster forebore on constitutional grounds to meddle:

The domestic slavery of the Southern States I leave where I find it, in the hands of their own governments. . . . I do not complain . . . it is the original bargain, the compact; let it stand; let the advantage of it [especially respecting southern representation in Congress] be fully enjoyed. The Union itself is too full of benefit to be hazarded in proposition for changing its original basis. I go for the Constitution as it is, and for the Union as it is.[15]

Webster then reviewed the history of New England's devotion to the Union and the region's concern for looking after national (including southern) interests as well as those at home. He paid special attention to refuting charges that he and New England had acted inconsistently on such matters, notably tariffs. "Shoulder to shoulder they went through the Revolution," he declared of Massachusetts and an earlier, more loyal South Carolina, "hand in hand they stood round the administration of Washington, and felt his own great arm lean on them for support." (vol. 6, pp. 49–50).

His replies to Hayne's insults made, Webster turned in the final third of his address to the Constitution, "to state, and to defend what I perceive to be the true principles of the Constitution." (vol. 6, p. 50). Bringing his legal skills to bear against Calhoun's theories, using arguments from his great court cases, Webster studied nullification in comparison with the Constitution. The question of nullification's validity depended on the nature of the Federal government. If the Union were "the creature of the State legislatures," Webster said that then nullification would in fact have a legal basis. But, he countered, "if it be the agent of the people, then the people alone can control it, restrain it, modify, or reform it." (vol. 6, p. 54). Webster insisted on this second definition and denied Calhoun's premises with language that would later inspire Abraham Lincoln:

It is, Sir,[16] the people's Constitution, the people's government, made for the people, made by the people, and answerable to the people. The people of the United States have declared that their Constitution shall be the supreme law . . . the state legislatures, however, sovereign as political bodies, are yet not sovereign over the people. . . . We are all agents of the same supreme power, the people.[17]

100

As described in this passage, the Constitution is very much a thing of man, a series of legal arrangements and ordinations contrived to meet specific human ends. Again of the Union:

> The people, then, Sir, erected this government. They gave it a Constitution, and in that Constitution they have enumerated the powers which they bestow on it. They have made it a limited government. They have defined its authority. They have restrained it to the exercise of such powers as are granted; and all others, they declare, are reserved to the States or the people. (vol. 6, p. 67).

Clearly, as Webster characterized it here, the constitutional Union was a device. Webster's rational argument in favor of its preservation was simply that the people had created it, and that the people objected to the termination of it by an outside agency, a state government. It follows from this that the Union was not imperishable, and that if they so chose, the people could dismantle their national government with serious but nonetheless largely political and economic consequences.

His legal and humanistic arguments made, Webster changed his strategy in the famous peroration, presenting the constitutional Union as something quite different. After holding forth at length with appeals to the Understanding, Webster began his appeal to the Will by assuming a pose straight out of Romantic poetry:

> I am conscious of having detained you and the Senate much too long. I was drawn into the debate without previous deliberation, such as is suited to the discussion of so grave and important a subject. But it is a subject of which my heart is full, and I have not been willing to suppress the utterance of its spontaneous sentiments. I cannot, even now, persuade myself to relinquish it, without expressing once more my deep conviction, that, since it respects nothing less than the Union of the States, it is of most vital and essential importance to the public happiness. (vol. 6, p. 74).

Even though reasonableness argued that he had made his case and that now he should speak no more, Webster simply could not suppress his heartfelt words—or so he claimed. he presented himself almost as a man possessed, who had no control over the emotions and "spontaneous sentiments" that demanded expression. The cause inspired him to poetry.

Webster called the Union "*vital* and *essential.*" As he had in earlier years, Webster gave credit for all of the country's success to the Union. "It is to that Union we own our safety at home, and our consideration and dignity abroad," he said; "it is to that Union, that we are chiefly indebted for whatever makes us most proud of our country." (vol. 6, p. 74). Although he had just spent several dozen pages explaining the human and legal character of the government, Webster here cast the Constitution and Union as the source and not only the means of national vitality.

Recalling the chaotic years of the Confederation, Webster continued his oratorical transformation: "That Union we reached only by the discipline of our virtues in the severe school of adversity. It had its origin in the necessities of disordered finance, prostrate commerce, and ruined credit. Under its benign influences, these great interests immediately awoke, as from the dead, and sprang forth with newness of life." (vol. 6, p. 24). Webster said two quite different things here. Prosaically, he traced the Union to economic, mundane matters and presented it as an agreement made by men with a specific set of problems to solve. But even as he did this, Webster immediately changed the Union from the result of cooperation and wisdom to their creator. With "benign influences," the Constitution awoke the nation from death. The new dispensation of republican liberty in unity perpetuated this sacred regeneration: "Every year of its duration teemed with fresh proofs of its utility and its blessings; and although our territory has stretched out wider and wider, and our population spread farther and farther, they have not outrun its protection or its benefits. It has been to us all a copious fountain of national, social, and personal happiness." (vol. 6, pp. 74–75). The government has "utility"—a passive quality. But it also offers "blessings," thereby taking on an active nature.

In contrast to these happy reflections, Webster pondered the consequences of nullification. Earlier in the speech he had rigorously explored the legal implications of Hayne's position; he analyzed how the different states would be irreconcilable if granted conflicting sovereignty, and he even imagined a scene from the actual event itself in which he pictured Hayne at the head of a South Carolina militia unit facing Federal troops. That grim and perplexing extrapolation may have sufficed for the prosaic part of Webster's defense of the Union and Constitution, but in the peroration he made his case in much more powerful, poetic terms. Although he had undeniably speculated on what would happen in post-nullification America, Webster now protested that he could never do so:

I have not allowed myself, Sir, to look beyond the Union, to see what might lie hidden in the dark recess behind. I have not coolly weighed the chances of preserving liberty when the bonds that unite us together shall be broken asunder. I have not accustomed myself to hang over the precipice of disunion, to see whether, with my short sight, I can fathom the depth of the abyss below . . . (vol. 6, p. 75).

"When we know the full extent of any danger," wrote Edmund Burke in his *A Philosophical Inquiry into the Origins of Our Ideas of the Sublime and Beautiful*, "when we can accustom our eyes to it, a great deal of the apprehension vanishes."[18] Since apprehension, the emotional counterpart to his logical persuasion, was key to Webster's strategy, the Defender of the Union refused in this passage to allow his listeners to accustom their eyes to disunion. He in fact warned them against any such calm consideration: "[N]or could I regard him as a safe counselor in the affairs of this government, whose thoughts should be mainly bent on considering, not how the Union may be best preserved, but how tolerable might be the condition of the people when it should be broken up and destroyed." (vol. 6. p. 75). Of course, in a deliberative body like the United States Senate, consideration of the sort that Webster forbid was entirely appropriate— but only in a rationalist context quite unlike that which Webster was creating in his peroration. He continued, presenting such speculation as a kind of hubristic blasphemy: "While the Union lasts, we have high, exciting, gratifying prospects spread out before us, for us and our children. Beyond that I seek not to penetrate the veil. God grant that in my day, at least, that curtain may not rise! God grant that on my vision never may be opened what lied behind!" (vol. 6, p. 75). In the Biblical sense implicit in Webster's prayer, "to pierce the veil" means to behold divine mysteries, visions perhaps glorious, but possibly horrifying to the mortal prophet. Again, even while he refused to describe disunion, Webster pictured it. He did so indirectly, though, imagining the scene from a heavenly perspective: "When my eyes shall be turned to behold for the last time the sun in heaven, may I not see him shining on the broken and dishonored fragments of a once glorious Union; on States disserved, discordant, belligerent; on a land rent with civil feuds, or drenched, it may be, with fraternal blood." (vol. 6, p. 75). Foreseeing the moment of his own death (at which, presumably, one sees beyond the earthly veil), Webster followed the nullified Union through secession, anger, and a war between brothers. Essentially a single-sentence poeticization of his earlier explication of the legal implications of the imagined battle of Charleston under Hayne's banner, this passage appealed potently to his listeners' and readers' emotions. Unlike its prosaic counterpart, which was filled with details and facts that could be questioned, this vision allowed for no rebuttal. Nullification came to mean not just administrative problems or even battle, but something much more fundamentally destructive of the Union as a super-human entity.

Webster countered this appalling scene with a happier prophecy. Instead of recalling his praise of the constitutional Union as a sound legal basis for national and local enterprises, Webster continued in the visionary mode:

> Let their [i.e., his eyes'] last and feeble lingering glance rather behold the glorious ensign of the republic, now known and honored throughout the earth, still full high advanced, its arms and trophies streaming in their original lustre, not a stripe erased or polluted, not a single star obscured, bearing for its motto, no such miserable interrogatory as "What is all this worth?" nor those words of delusion and folly, "Liberty first and Union afterwards"; but everywhere, spread all over in characters of living light, blazing on all its ample folds, as they float over the sea and over the land, and in every wind under the whole heavens, that other sentiment, dear to every true American heart—Liberty *and* Union, now and for ever, one and inseparable! (vol. 6, p. 75).

While his picture of disunion was dark and slow to emerge even as indistinctly as he allowed himself to portray it in the peroration, Webster's blazing icon of Union was visible to all. The sun in heaven could only watch helplessly while the country collapsed, but the splendid flag would dispel the darkness of nullification. Usually the sun is itself an image of life and safety, but Webster replaced it with his flag. Ubiquitous and immortal, it flies over the entire world, shining "now and for ever," blazing with a living light. Represented by this symbol, the Constitution and Union are objects of the highest veneration.

Although it did not end the nullification debate or save the country from exactly the bloody fate he imagined for it, "The Second Reply to Hayne" did have profound effects on Webster himself. Henceforth he was known as the Defender of the Constitution, the Champion of the Union, and by other similar epithets. In the years that followed, partly out of genuine conviction and no doubt as well because the issue served him handily in politics, Webster returned to the cause of the Union time and time again. He did not abandon his legal line of argument (the 1833 "The Constitution not a Compact between Sovereign States" is a masterful example of this strategy), but he did rely more and more on his poetry of the Constitution and Union. Marking the centennial of Washington's birth in 1832, Webster took subtextual shots at nullification by attributing the Union to a messianic first President. Awarded a vase by Boston citizens for his work on behalf of the Union, he praised the government first as "a balanced and guarded system," then as an object for perpetual and global admiration.[19] Speaking to a crowd of New York merchants at Niblo's Saloon in 1837, Webster discoursed on the financial benefits of the Union, describing its potential fall as the collapse of a sacred temple into "melancholy and ruins."[20] Stumping for Henry Clay in 1844, he told an Albany audience that the Constitution was a commerical compact, but then characterized it as "the ark of our safety [which] gave a new significance and a new respect to the power-imparting name of America: on the foundation we still rest."[21] And in Savannah, Georgia, as part of his own abortive campaign for the Whig nomination, Webster called the Union both "the results of concessions and compromises" and a "family," an emotionally bound unit.[22]

Twenty years after his "Reply to Hayne," Webster delivered another series of Union speeches, once again denying the separate states the power of ignoring Federal law. In the 1830s, Webster attacked the South Carolina nullifiers; in the 1850s, he chastened his own people for their resistance to the Fugitive Slave Law that played such an important part in Clay's Compromise Measures. Coming at the end of his life and at a time when civil war seemed a very real possibility, this two years' worth of speeches epitomize Webster's constitutional rhetoric. Appealing to law and the Constitution, he argued that Northerners had no right to "nullify" the Fugitive Slave Law by refusing to allow its enforcement. Following this line of attack, Webster frequently rejected the abolitionists' claim that they were obeying "a higher law" like that invoked by Wendell Phillips when he spoke of Elder Brewster sending rifles to Kansas. As we saw in the 1850 "Pilgrim Festival at New York" address, Webster wanted religion to stay out of politics. He stated this clearly in his keynote address for the Compromise Measures, "The Constitution and the Union" (also known as "The Seventh of March").

Like "The Second Reply to Hayne," "The Constitution and the Union" consists in the main of tough factual argument. Always bringing his analysis back to the Constitution and basing his arguments on it, Webster reviewed the history of the crisis. He recalled how California first attracted settlers and finally came into the Union free of slavery, then discoursed on slavery, disagreement over which he saw as the immediate cause of the trouble. Tracing it back to Rome and earlier, Webster decried slavery on moral grounds, but defended its limited existence as guaranteed by the Constitution. He noted that "upon the general nature and influence of slavery, there exists a wide difference of opinion between the northern portion of this country and the southern."[23] In the North, he explained, the main objection took its inspiration from religion. Abolitionist opinions "have taken hold of the religious sentiment of that part of the country." (vol. 10, p. 62). And, "when a question of this kind seizes on the religious sentiments of mankind, and comes to be discussed in religious assemblies of the clergy and laity, there is always to be expected, or always to be feared, a great deal of excitement." (vol. 10, p. 63).

Webster's insistence that religion not be allowed to interfere with law is especially striking in view of how he had long used poetic language to create something akin to a religion of the American constitutional Union. The practice began as early as his 1802 warning that "Miracles do not cluster." "The Constitution and Union" does not include much of Webster's mythic Constitution, but despite his complaints in that address about people basing their decisions and actions on emotional and spiritual inclinations, Webster made religious language and strategies a central part of his work for the Union at this time.

The classic example is "The Addition to the Capitol," Webster's last Independence Day address, which he delivered in 1851 at a ceremonial laying of the cornerstone for a new wing of the Capitol building. The speech opens with a wonderful passage that reads more like the words of a prophet than of a constitutional lawyer. "Hail! All hail!" Webster greeted the crowd;

I see before and around me a mass of faces, glowing with cheerfulness and patriotic pride. I see thousands of eyes turned towards other eyes, all sparkling with gratification and delight. This is the New World! This is America! This is Washington! and this the Capitol of the United States! And where else, among the nations, can the seat of government be surrounded, on any day in any year, by those who have more reason to rejoice in the blessings which they possess? Nowhere, fellow-citizens! assuredly, nowhere! Let us, then, meet this rising sun with joy and thanksgiving.

This is that day of the year which announced to mankind the great fact of American Independence. This fresh and brilliant morning blesses our vision with another beholding of the birthday of our nation.[24]

We hear almost an ecstatic tone in Webster's vision of America. Overwhelmed by the immediacy and presence of the Union's blessings, he spoke as one on fire with inspiration.

His celebration of the New World, of "this rising sun," and of the "fresh and brilliant morning [which] bless our vision" recalls the morning of Christ's nativity, or perhaps the first glimpse of the regenerated world after the Second Coming. In this passage, all the earlier suggestions that the Constitution and Union marked a new dispensation with spiritual as well as political significance reach a new development. He continued in the prophetic vein by looking back to the early days of settlement. He cited Bishop Berkeley's "Verses on the Prospect of planting Arts and learning in America:"

> Westward the course of empire takes its way;
>   The four first acts already past,
> A fifth shall close the drama with the day:
>   Time's noblest offspring is the last. (vol. 4, p. 294).

Calling this verse an "extraordinary prophecy," Webster said, "So clear a vision of what America would become . . . was an intuitive glance into futurity; it was a grand conception, strong, ardent, glowing, embracing all time since the creation of the world . . . (vol. 4, p. 294).

Webster spoke for a few moments about the Declaration of Independence, stressing not so much the revolutionary character of independence as he did its function as a force for national unity. "This anniversary animates and gladdens and unites all American hearts," he said in words recalling the peroration to "The Second Reply." "On other days we may be party men . . . [b]ut today we are Americans all; and all nothing but Americans. As the great luminary over our heads, dissipating mists and fogs, now cheers the whole hemisphere, so do the associations connected with this day disperse all cloudy and sullen weather in the minds and hearts of true Americans." (vol. 4, p. 297). Contemplating liberty in its various political forms through the ages, Webster concluded that neither Greece nor Rome nor any other country had enjoyed liberty as great as America's. He attributed "true constitutional liberty" to five things: representative (and specifically *not* pure) democracy; majority rule; the supremacy of law over all; the existence of a constitution "founded on the immediate authority of the people themselves, and regulating and restraining all the powers conferred upon government"; and public virtue. (vol. 4, p. 300). Notice that each of these involves restraint and obedience—exactly the qualities that Webster believed necessary to preserve the Union.

And so Webster turned to his constant subject, the Union and its perpetuation. First he offered factual arguments in its favor—statistics about population and wealth that he called "infallible proof of the growth and prosperity of the nation," and then he came to his point: "I ask you, and I would ask every man, whether the government which has been over us has proved itself an affliction or a curse to the country, or any part of it." (vol. 4, p. 305). Obviously, Webster answered, "No," and he did so by slipping into a religious mode, using the first of three remarkable Biblical references that appear in the speech. It is to Matthew 23:31, in which Christ attacked the Pharisees for failing to see that the prophecies of old were coming true: "Ye men of the South, of all the original Southern states, what say you to all this? Are you, or any of you, ashamed of this work? Your fathers were not they who stoned the prophets and killed them. They were among the prophets: they were of the prophets; they were themselves the prophets." (vol. 4, p. 305). Webster transformed the politicians, statesmen, and lawyers who contrived the Constitution and Union into Old Testament prophets. Christ's next line (not quoted by Webster) would also have been appropriate: "Fill ye up then the measure of your fathers." Failure to honor and obey the Constitution as

Webster interpreted it here became in this allegory not only filial disloyalty, but apostasy.

Speaking of the return to national harmony that he hoped for, Webster used another Biblical story, the parable of the Prodigal Son. "Fellow citizens," he said, "there are some diseases of the mind as well as of the body, diseases of communities as well as diseases of individuals, that must be left to their own cure; at least it is wise to leave them so until the last critical moment shall arrive." (vol. 4, pp. 306–307). Webster's common depiction of the Union as one big family took on special significance when he told of the Prodigal Son:

He had broken away from all the ties of love, family, and friendship. He had forsaken every thing which he had once regarded in his father's house. He had forsworn his natural sympathies, affections, and habits, and taken his journey into a far country. . . . [M]isfortunes overtook him, and famine threatened with starvation and death. . . . But the hour of reflection had come, and nature and conscience wrought within him, until at length "he came to himself." (vol. 4, p. 307).

This little parable is packed with implications. First, Webster made loyalty to the Union a matter of deep familial kinship, of "natural sympathies" and even of sanity, in that disloyalty makes the son something other than himself. Second, the religious context of the story reinforces Webster's portrayal of the Union as something much more than a human government. He could easily have used any number of non-Biblical parallels to make his point, and his reference to the parable of the Prodigal Son reveals much about his rhetorical strategy and about how he wanted people to see themselves in relation to the government.

Webster followed the parable with a third Biblical reference, one recalling the final scene of "The Second Reply to Hayne" and also the bright opening of "The Addition to the Capitol". Concluding the speech, Webster vowed, "We cannot, we dare not, we will not, betray our sacred trust," and prophesied that the nation would survive:

The bow that gilds the clouds in the heavens, the pillars, that uphold the firmament, may disappear and fall away in the hour appointed by the will of God; but until that day comes, or so long as our lives may last, no ruthless hand shall undermine that bright arch of Union and Liberty which spans the continent from Washington to California. (vol. 4, p. 317).

In the Bible, the rainbow was God's sign to his chosen people of the Covenant. The "arch of Union" stood in Webster's iconography for the Constitution—the new covenant that had created the United States.

5. The Spirit of the Age

Earlier I suggested that Daniel Webster helped cause the Civil War, the very disaster that he worked so hard to prevent. He did so in part with his constitutional arguments in favor of a strong central government, and by his support of various measures (such as tariffs or the Fugitive Slave Law) that aggravated sectional differences. Five hundred thousand Americans died not over taxes, nor even over the necessary crusade to end slavery, but for the preservation of the Union. The Confederates may have seceded because they wanted to escape Federal interference with their laws and institutions, but Lincoln fought the war with a single paramount goal. As he wrote to Horace Greeley in August of 1862, a month after he drafted a proclamation to free slaves in the Confederacy (but not in Maryland or Delaware, which stayed in the Union even though they were slave states),

> I would save the Union. I would save it the shortest way under the Constitution. The sooner the National authority can be restored, the nearer the Union will be "the Union as it was." If there be those who would not save the Union unless they could at the same time *save* Slavery, I do not agree with them. If there be those who would not save the Union unless they could at the same time *destroy* Slavery, I do not agree with them. My paramount object in this struggle *is* to save the Union, and is *not* either to save or destroy Slavery. If I could save the Union without freeing *any* slave, I would do it; and if I could do it by freeing *all* slaves, I would do it; and if I could do it by freeing some and leaving others alone, I would also do that. What I do about Slavery and the colored race, I do because I believe it helps to save this Union; and what I forbear, I forbear because I do *not* believe it would help to save the Union.[1]

Why, we should ask, did the preservation of the Union under the Constitution mean so much—enough that Lincoln would suffer slavery to exist despite his profound loathing of it, and enough to send Union armies raging into the South? Part of the answer lies in the words of Daniel Webster, in his poetic interpretations of the Constitution and its meanings, and in his prophetic visions of disunion. We have seen how Webster made America's past the stuff of mythology and how he translated his legal doctrines into something quite akin to a religion. When he spoke of the future, Webster treated possible scenarios in the same way that he did the settlement and establishment of the nation.

Speaking in his prosaic or lawyerly voice, Webster frequently discussed the ramifications of fragmentation as administrative, legal, and even military quandaries. "The Second Reply to Hayne" concludes twice, first with rigorous analysis of what nullification might mean in real terms. Running "the honorable gentleman's doctrine a little bit into its practical application," Webster compared the confusion of America with nullification to the country's condition under the old

Articles of Confederation.[2] He extrapolated from the debate to a military scene, imagining Hayne himself (in his capacity as an officer of the South Carolina militia) pulled into a chain of actions and reactions leading to confrontation with Federal troops. "This," said Webster, "is war,—civil war. Direct collision, therefore, between force and force, is the unavoidable result of that remedy for the revision of certain unconstitutional laws which the gentleman contends for." (vol. 6, p. 71). This is serious talk, and no doubt gave potential supporters of Hayne and Calhoun pause. But in the second conclusion to the speech, the splendid peroration with its vision of "the sun shining on the broken and dishonored fragments of a once glorious Union," (vol. 6, p. 75), Webster translated his straightforward and reasonably effective analysis into an apocalyptic revelation. As explained prosaically, nullification meant confusion and the possibility of armed strife; as expressed in the peroration, it promised the destruction of the American dream, a scene so horrific that ordinary language could not capture it.

"The Character of Washington," the 1832 dinner address in which Webster beatified Washington as a Unionist saint, also pictured the fall of America with moving imagery. Declaring that the collapse of the Capitol building itself would be only a minor calamity capable of repair, Webster expanded his architectural motif. "But who shall reconstruct the fabric of demolished government," he asked:

Who shall rear again the well-proportioned columns of constitutional liberty? Who shall frame together the skilful architecture which unifies national sovereignty with State rights, individual security and public prosperity? No, if these columns fall, they will be raised not again. Like the Coliseum and the Parthenon, they will be destined to a mournful, a melancholy immortality. Bitterer tears, however, will flow over them, than were ever shed over the monuments of Roman and Grecian art; for they will be the remnants of a more glorious edifice than Greece or Rome ever saw, the edifice of Constitutional American liberty.[3]

Webster often compared the United States to its ancient models, Greece and Rome. "The First Settlement of New England" and "The Addition to the Capitol" are two instances in which he explicitly praised American liberty and republicanism. "The State of Our Literature" and "The Dignity and Importance of History," with their implicitly valued aesthetic, called for a new kind of art for the new republic. Great though the accomplishments of the ancients may have been, they paled in Webster's rhetoric next to the glories of the American Union. He contrasted the physical ruins of the past—the Coliseum and the Parthenon—not to the actual buildings of the United States, but to the intangible fragments of "constitutional American liberty." Implying that Americans worked on a higher, more philosophical plane than the ancients did, Webster saw in the establishment of the United States the beginning of a new moral and political dispensation for humanity. Along with his characterization of George Washington as a global hero, Webster also presented America as the leader of a new age for civilization. Greek and Roman architects worked in stone and mortar; Americans created a social edifice far beyond those old ruins.

A later version of this image was even more striking. Speaking to supporters at Niblo's Saloon in 1837, he again depicted the break-up of the Union as the collapse of a great building. Predicting that "the noble idea of United American Liberty, of *our* liberty, such as our fathers established it [would] be extinguished forever," Webster imagined the end of the country.[4] "Fragments and shattered columns of the edifice may be found remaining; and melancholy and mournful ruins they will be," he said; "The august temple itself will be prostrate in the dust." (vol. 2, p. 199). The American Union was both the national religion and its own temple in this allegory. Combining the spiritual and administrative aspects of the government, he made loyalty to the form equal to—and not merely necessary for—devotion to the ends of government as he believed Washington had established it. This mystical transubstantiation was a strong if curious buttress for the Union.

Perhaps Webster's most well-known use of such a metaphor came in his Bunker Hill monument speeches. In "The Bunker Hill Monument" speech of 1825, the first of two that he would deliver, Webster echoed his 1800 description of the government as "the greatest approximation towards human perfection the political world ever yet experienced."[5] With veterans of the Revolution listening, Webster again spoke of the United States government as something with extra-legal importance. He described the Union as a memorial for the Revolutionary generation, and speaking of the obelisk under construction behind him, Webster used an image that captured his hopes for both the country and the stone monument:

> The foundation of that monument we have now laid. With solemnities suited to the occasion, with prayers to Almighty God for his blessing and in the midst of this cloud [sic] of witnesses, we have begun the work. We trust that it will be prosecuted, and that, springing from a broad foundation, rising high in massive solidity and unadorned grandeur, it may remain as long as Heaven permits the works of man to last, a fit emblem, both of the events in memory of which it is raised, and of the gratitude of those who have reared it.[6]

Webster had begun his speech by calling his "the early age of this great continent." (vol. 1, p. 235). The great task of that era, he suggested through the analogy of the Union, was the building of a national foundation. Webster referred throughout the speech to the Union in words that stressed "massive solidity." He spoke of the colonies working together and of the growing fraternity of the states. Just as they had begun a stone obelisk that would rise in strength, so had Americans begun to build the Union. At the end of his

117

speech, Webster made these hints and allusions clear. "Let us cultivate a true spirit of union and harmony," he said;

In pursuing the great objects which our condition points out to us, let us act under a settled conviction, and an habitual feeling, that these twenty-four States are one country. . . . Let our object be OUR COUNTRY, OUR WHOLE COUNTRY, AND NOTHING BUT OUR COUNTRY. And, by the blessing of God, may that country itself become a vast and splendid monument, not of oppression and terror, but of Wisdom, of Peace, and of Liberty, upon which the world may gaze with admiration for ever! (vol. 1, p. 254).

Webster turned the Union into an icon of itself. Even if the nation might have started as a series of legal measures to achieve particular goals, Webster's visionary rhetoric transformed it into a symbol and an entity of greater significance. Presumably, in this speech, the legal Union was but a foundation for its spiritual complement.

In 1843, with the debate over Texas spurring sectional tempers, Webster returned to Charleston to celebrate the completion of the Bunker Hill monument. Again he made the obelisk rising behind him the central image of the speech and the linchpin of his rhetorical strategy. "This column stands on Union," he said;

I know that it might not keep its position if the American Union in the mad conflict of human passions, and in the strife of parties and factions, should be broken up and destroyed. I know not that it would totter and fall to the earth, and mingle its fragments with the fragments of Liberty and the Constitution, when State should be separated from State and faction and dismemberment obliterate forever all the hope of the founders of our republic, and the great inheritance.[7]

The monument served, to use Eliot's phrase, as Webster's objective correlative. As the scene of a torn and blood-soaked land made concrete the dangers of nullification in "The Second Reply to Hayne," so would the fall of the obelisk express disunion in this vision. Webster suggested that the

118

monument might in fact not crumble if the Union did, and added another aspect to his metaphor: "It might stand. But who, from beneath the weight of mortification and shame that would oppress him, could look up to behold it? Whose eyeballs would not be seared by such a spectacle? For my part, should I live to such a time, I shall avert my eyes from it forever." (vol. 1, pp. 266–267). Even though this second image was more realistic in that the column would not collapse through some mysterious sympathy, it had just as strong an emotional significance in and of itself. The fall of republican liberty would still leave fragments burying Americans. To this disaster, Webster juxtaposed the solid column, now representing the failure of Americans to live up to the ideals that had inspired its construction. Recalling his fear to view the broken Union in "The Second Reply," Webster averted his eyes from the potential symbol of his country's shame. "Woe betide the man who brings to this day's worship feeling less than wholly American," (vol. 1, p. 265), he warned. Looking upon such a holy icon with secessionist eyes was blasphemy.

Webster also used images from nature to express his fear of disunion in its various forms. At Concord, New Hampshire in 1834, he called the Constitution the sun of the Union and prophesied that without it Americans would "grope out in darkness and despair the remainder of a miserable existence."[8] He expanded this scene of natural desolation for a Capon Springs, Virginia audience in 1851. "[S]ecession and disunion are a region of gloom," he said, "and morass and swamp; no cheerful breezes fan it, no spirit of health visits it; it is all malaria. It is all fever and ague. Nothing beautiful or useful grows in it; the traveller through it breathes miasma, and treads among all things unwholesome and loathsome."[9] In accord with this motif, Webster often described the American mission as a voyage through a world of dangers. At

Bangor, Maine in 1835, he said that while the nation could withstand "an enormous load of official mismanagement," it could never survive any shock to the Union.[10] Should the ship of state split apart, he said, "she will lie on the billows helpless and hopeless, the scorn and contempt of all the enemies of free institutions, and an object of indescribable grief to all her friends." (vol. 2, p. 165). The opening of "The Constitution and the Union" is an especially good example of the voyage motif:

The imprisoned winds are let loose. The East, the North, and the stormy South combine to throw the whole sea into commotion, to toss its billows to the skies, and disclose its profoundest depths. I do not affect to regard myself, Mr. President, as holding, or as fit to hold, the helm in this combat with the political elements; but I have a duty to perform, and I mean to perform it with fidelity, not without a sense of existing dangers, but not without hope. I have a part to act, not for my own security or safety, for I am looking out for no fragment upon which to float away from the wreck, if wreck there must be, but for the good of the whole and the preservation of all; and there is that which will keep me to my duty during this struggle, whether the sun and stars shall appear, or shall not appear for many days. I speak today for the preservation of the Union.[11]

Even though he feared calamity, Webster always offered and stressed a positive alternative to his grim prophecies. Since the fate of the nation would depend on decisions and votes by individual citizens and legislators, he gave clear choices, emphasizing that his listeners would bear responsibility for the outcome. He made them characters in the story that he told about America's past and future—whether heroes or villains, he left to them. The promise of a happy ending always existed. Just as he resolved "The Second Reply to Hayne" by banishing gloom with his vision of the omnipresent flag, so did Webster answer his images of swamps, storms, and ship-wrecked voyages with happier prospects. "The Constitution and The Union," for example, responded to the miasmic mood of entrapment in the Capon Springs speech: "And now, Mr. President, instead of speaking of the possibility or utility of secession, instead of dwelling in those caverns of darkness, groping with those ideas so full of all that is horrid and horrible, let us come out into the light of day; let us enjoy the fresh air of liberty and Union." (vol. 10, p. 97).

A classic example concludes "The Dignity and Importance of History," the contrived myth-history that Webster delivered in 1852 to support his Unionism. Having finished his story of America's past, Webster told his listeners that they "must forget the things which are behind, and act with immoveable firmness, like a band of brothers, with moderation and conciliation, forgetting past disagreements and looking only to the great object set before them—the preservation bequeathed to them by their ancestors. They must gird up their loins for the work."[12] He denied assertions that the Union could be reorganized by a new plan, and used a powerful cosmological image to make his point:

I no more believe it possible that this Union, should it once be dissolved, could ever be returned, and all the states reassociated, than I believe it possible that, if, by the fiat of the Almighty power, the law of gravitation should be abolished, and the orbs which compose the Universe should rush into illimitable space, jostling against each other, they could be brought back and readjusted into harmony by any new principle of attraction. (vol. 13, p. 496).

The end, if it came, would come swiftly and with no escape. Webster shifted from his astronomical image to a Biblical one. Substituting the name of America for that of Babylon, he quoted from the Book of Revelations:

We shall die no lingering death. We shall fall victims to neither war, pestilence, nor famine. An earthquake would shake the foundations of the globe, pull down the pillars of heaven, and bury us at once in endless darkness. Such may be the fate of the country and its institutions. May

121

I never live to see that day! May I not survive to hear any apocalyptic angel crying through the heavens, with such a voice as announced the fall of Babylon, [America the great is fallen, is fallen, and is become the habitation of devils, and the hold of every foul spirit, and a cage of every unclean and hateful bird.] (vol. 13, p. 496).[13]

But of course, Webster balanced this vision of the world's end with another vision, a pastoral of faith and joy, ending his speech on an optimistic note by celebrating the birthday of George Washington: "The whole atmosphere is redolent of his name: hills and forests, racks and rivers, echo and reecho his praises." (vol. 13, p. 496). If true to Washington and his Unionism, Americans could safely walk through the valley of the shadow of secessionism and pass into glory:

To that standard, we shall adhere, and uphold it, through evil report and through good report. We will meet danger, we will meet death, if they come in, in its protection; and we will struggle on, in daylight and in darkness, aye, in the thickest darkness, with all the storms which it may bring with it, till
"Danger's troubled night is o'er,
And the star of Peace return." (vol. 13, p. 497).

Why, other than to avoid the war and other dangers that he imagined (or to give him a good issue on which to base his political career) did Daniel Webster preach so passionately that the Union had to survive? What was the meaning of America to Daniel Webster? In the answer to these questions lies the greater importance of Webster's beatific visions, Webster's dream of the United States as an economic and civic success on its own, as the prophet of a global revolution, and as the ultimate stage in God's millennial scheme for humanity.

On numerous occasions, Webster told his countrymen of their successes. On the one hand were their accomplishments at home, the triumph of civilization over the natural wilderness. On a tour of frontier states in 1837, Webster com-

THE SPIRIT OF THE AGE

plimented St. Louis and predicted greater things to come. "How little could the most sanguine temperament have looked forward to an hour like this," he said; "Where once was wilderness, I have beheld the comforts, the luxuries, the refinements of polished existence. Who shall speak, then, of glory for the future?"[14] All of this material achievement argued for the preservation of the national government under which it had occurred. However, Webster spoke even more forcefully about the American mission to humanity, the spiritual counterpart to its financial wealth. Three speeches in particular epitomize Webster's definition of this calling, "The Revolution in Greece" (1824), "The Bunker Hill Monument" (1825), and one from his later years, "The Festival of the Sons of New Hampshire" (1849). Manifesting different aspects of the national character and reflecting the circumstances of their separate times of composition, these speeches are poetic masterpieces. Short on specific advice for action, they all embody Webster's sense of America as a moral force.

Delivered in sympathy for a rebellion against the Turkish empire, "The Revolution in Greece" offered little substantive aid to the Greeks. Far from suggesting intervention or even the provision of arms or of funds for arms, Webster merely moved that Congress allocate money for a Presidential agent to visit Greece. From this small start, though, Webster went on to define his own country's role rather grandly. "I cannot forget the age in which we live," he said, "the pervading spirit of the age, the interesting questions which agitate it, and our own peculiar relation to these interesting questions."[15] The rebellion was for all practical purposes only Webster's pretext so that he could talk about America and the new age:

The Age is extraordinary. The civilized world has done with "the enormous faith, of many made for one." Society asserts its own rights, and alleges

123

them to be original, sacred, and unalienable. It is not satisfied with having kind masters; it demands a participation in its own government; and in states much advanced in civilization, it urges this demand with a constancy and an energy that cannot well nor long be resisted. (vol. 5, p. 70).

The attitudes of Turkey and the Holy Alliance flew in the face of the spirit of the age, "promulgating doctrines and fraught with consequences wholly subversive in their tendency of the public law of nations and of the general liberties of mankind." (vol. 5, p. 67). Appalled at the indifference shown by European nations to the Alliance, Webster called on the United States to lead the free world—not quite the first time that Americans had heard this call (it is as old as the Puritan sermons), and far from the last. "Our history, our situation, our character," he said, "necessarily decide our position and our course, before we have even time to ask whether we have an option." (vol. 5, p. 66). Webster told Americans that they would be the great new power in an era dominated by a new kind of might: moral opinion.

The 1825 "Bunker Hill Monument" address developed this theme more completely. Noting once again the uniqueness of the age and asserting that the United States led it, Webster sang the glories of mankind's improved moral and intellectual condition:

The whole world is becoming a common field for intellect to act in. Mind is the great lever of all things; human thought is the process by which human ends are ultimately answered; and the diffusion of knowledge, so astonishing in the last half-century, has rendered innumerable minds, variously gifted by nature, competent to be competitors or fellow-workers on the theatre of intellectual operation. (vol. 1, p. 247).

With knowledge enlightening the world as "the great sun in the firmament"—an echo of how he spoke sometimes of the Union and the Constitution—, Webster predicted peace for humanity and traced this new era directly to the founding of the American government. "Government," he said, "is the master topic of the age; and during the whole fifty years [since 1776] it has intensely occupied the thoughts of men." (vol. 1, p. 248). Thanks to what Americans had achieved through their politics, Webster declared, "a real, substantial, and important change has taken place, and is taking place, highly favorable, on the whole, to human happiness." (vol. 1, p. 248). The Founding Fathers had initiated a world-wide millennium, exemplified by what Webster saw in South America:

[I]n our day there has been, as it were a new creation. The Southern hemisphere emerges from the sea. Its lofty mountains begin to lift themselves into the sight of heaven; its broad and fertile plains stretch out, in beauty, to the eye of civilized man, and at the mighty bidding of the voice of political liberty the waters of darkness retire. (vol. 1, p. 252).

Webster described nothing less than a new age, one in which human political innovations surpassed divine creation of the world itself, a paradise for a race created not in the image of Jehovah, but in that of George Washington and his fellows.

"The Festival of the Sons of New Hampshire" is an exceptionally good speech from November, 1849, just a few months prior to "The Constitution and The Union." Distressed about the tensions between North and South, Webster combined exhortations for the constitutional Union with his gospel of America's duty to humanity. The first half of the speech centered on New Hampshire, its history and its people. (The Sons of New Hampshire consisted of Bostonians either born in New Hampshire or descended from citizens of that state.) Running through the settlement, the wars with the Indians and the French, Webster praised the "[m]anly strength, the nerved arm of freemen, each one tilling his own land, and standing on his own soil, enjoying what he earns, and ready to defend it."[16] Yet for all that he said about the state's independence and grit, Webster predictably constructed his

THE POETRY OF EVENTS

history to show how it contributed to the formation and maintenance of the Union. With this accomplished, Webster paused while others spoke to the crowd (chiefly by delivering toasts, which must also have helped prepare the audience for Webster's inspiring words on the Constitution).

"Gentlemen," he said, returning to the floor,

"departing from the character of particular States, leaving for the present the agreeable thoughts that have entertained us, of our own homes, and our own origin, . . . we should call to our attention the marked character of the age in which we live, and the great part that, in the dispensations of Divine Providence, we are called upon to act in it." (vol. 4, p. 206).

Calling his "an age of progress . . . towards self-government," Webster identified the paramount question of the era as "how this impulse can be carried on, without running to excess; how popular government can be established, without falling into licentiousness." (vol. 4, p. 209). Ostensibly talking about foreign nations whose revolutions went to dangerous extremes, Webster was really pointing a warning finger at those Americans who put conscience or the rights of single states above duty to the Federal Constitution. Dismissing the "common sentiment uttered by those who would revolutionize Europe, that, to be free, men only have to *will* it," (vol. 4, p. 209), Webster saw two fundamental principles: representative government, and an absolute obedience of that government and its laws. "To abide by the voice of the representatives fairly chosen," he said, "by the edicts of those who make the legislative enactments, has been and is our only system." (vol. 4, p. 209). We are accustomed to hearing our leaders praise our freedom, but Webster emphasized obedience. Obviously, Webster was telling people, abolitionists and secessionists alike, that they must heed the Constitutional restraints. To do otherwise threatened not only domestic stability, but the fate of the earth:

We are bound to show to the whole world, in the midst of which we are placed, that a regular, steady, conservative government, founded on broad, popular, representative systems, is a practicable thing. . . . [O]ur mission is to show that a constitutional, representative, conservative government, founded on the freest possible principles, can do, *can do,* for the advancement of general morals and the general prosperity, as much as any other government can do. This is our business, this our mission among the nations; and it is a nobler destiny, even, than that which Virgil assigns to imperial Rome. (vol. 4, pp. 208 and 211).

Webster centered his closing remarks on the revolt of Hungary against Austria. Saying that the United States could stand up and protest on behalf of the rebels only so long as it held true to its own political creed—i.e., Unionism—, Webster urged his countrymen to "consider the mission and destiny which Providence seems to have designed for us." (vol. 4, p. 213). Webster did not care enormously about Hungary, and his remarks seem to have had more to do with troubles at home than abroad. Puffing up the country's sense of itself as a moral force in the modern world, Webster argued that helping Hungary, along with all of the country's other achievements, depended on maintaining the integrity of the Union.

Despite the hints of gloom in his last speeches, hints born perhaps of desperation and subtextually present in the catastrophic imagery that he so insistently (and frequently) denied, Daniel Webster wanted very much to believe in the future of the United States. Founded in a mythic past, raised to glorious heights in the eyes of the world, the Union could lead humanity to a new age. In 1820, Webster called on his countrymen to make their land a link in the great chain of civilization "which begins with the origin of our race, runs onward through its successive generations, binding together the past, the present, and the future, and terminating at last, with the consummation of all things earthly at the throne of God."[17] Twenty years after he spoke those words in

Plymouth, Webster pleaded with Whigs at a convention in Richmond, "Let us discuss with moderation and coolness the great topics of policy, and endeavor to bring all men of American heart and feeling into what I sincerely believe to be the true AMERICAN CAUSE."[18] Echoing his Plymouth speech, Webster equated the American government with Creation itself:

> I cannot find a deeper or more fervent sentiment in my heart than that these precious institutions and liberties which we enjoy may be transmitted unimpaired to the latest posterity; that they may terminate only with the termination of all things earthly, when the world itself shall terminate,
> "When, wrapped in flames, the
>   realms of ether glow,
> And Heaven's last thunders
>   shake the world below." (vol. 3, p. 102).

What should we make of Daniel Webster's poetic language? Was it mere eloquence that inspired Americans to fight a terrible war not for objective reasons, but out of devotion to an artificial, literary myth? After reading all of Webster's speeches and concentrating on their visionary aspects, I think that the source of his power is how he combined his legal and poetic voices. Webster did more than just amass factual evidence and then present it felicitously. With the genius of an epic poet, Webster made narrative sense of America for his listeners and readers, translating his prosaic understanding of the world into something more accessible, universal, and certainly more moving. Despite their successes, Americans have always felt a curious cultural and political anxiety about their survival and their purpose. In Webster's day, the young republic fit well Ernst Cassirer's description of a culture in crisis. "In the critical moments of man's political and social life," Cassirer wrote in 1944, "myth regains its old strength."[19] Eulogizing John Adams in 1826, Webster spoke of "true eloquence." "The clear conception," he declared, outrunning the deductions of logic, the high purpose, the firm resolve, the dauntless spirit, speaking on the tongue, beaming from the eye, informing every feature, and urging the whole man onward, right onward to his object,—this, this is eloquence; or rather it is something greater and higher than all eloquence, it is action, noble, sublime, god-like action.[20]

Often called "the God-like Daniel," perhaps Webster earned that epithet because of his own talent for using belief and imagination to reconstitute human law and history into myth and poetry.

Notes

Introduction

1. Rufus Choate, "A Discourse Commemorative of Daniel Webster, Delivered before the Faculty, Students, and Alumni of Dartmouth College, July 27, 1853," *Addresses and Orations of Rufus Choate* (Boston: Little, Brown, 1897), p. 295.

2. Ibid., p. 296.

3. Ibid., p. 297.

4. George Ticknor Curtis, *Life of Daniel Webster,* 2 vols. (New York: D. Appleton, 1870).

5. Claude Fuess, *Daniel Webster,* 2 vols. (Boston: Little, Brown, 1930).

6. Richard Current, *Daniel Webster and the Rise of National Conservatism* (Boston: Little, Brown, 1955).

7. Irving Bartlett, *Daniel Webster* (New York: W.W. Norton, 1978); Maurice Baxter, *One and Inseparable: Daniel Webster and the Union* (Cambridge: Harvard University Press, 1984).

8. Maurice Baxter, *Daniel Webster and the Supreme Court* (Amherst: University of Massachusetts Press, 1966).

9. Norman D. Brown, *Daniel Webster and the Politics of Availability* (Athens: University of Georgia Press, 1969).

10. Sydney Nathans, *Daniel Webster and Jacksonian Democracy* (Baltimore: Johns Hopkins University Press, 1973).

11. Robert F. Dalzell, Jr., *Daniel Webster and the Trial of American Nationalism, 1843–1852* (Boston: Houghton Mifflin, 1973).

12. Edwin Percy Whipple, "Daniel Webster as a Master of English Style," *American Literature and Other Papers* (Boston: Houghton Mifflin, 1899).

13. Wilbur Samuel Howell and Hoyt Hopewell Hudson, "Daniel Webster," William Norwood Brigance, ed., *A History and Criticism of American Public Address*, 2 vols. (New York: McGraw-Hill, 1942), vol. 2, pp. 665–733.

14. Paul C. Nagel, *One Nation Indivisible: The Union in American Thought, 1776–1861* (New York: Oxford University Press, 1964); *This Sacred Trust: American Nationality, 1789–1898* (New York: Oxford University Press, 1971).

15. Ferenc M. Szasz, "Daniel Webster—Architect of America's 'Civil Religion'," *Historical New Hampshire*, 34, 3 & 4 (Fall/Winter, 1979), pp. 236–257.

16. Robert A. Ferguson, "Daniel Webster: Counsel for the Defense," *Law and Letters in American Culture* (Cambridge: Harvard University Press, 1984), pp. 207–240.

Chapter One

1. J. Thomas Stevenson, Introduction to "Speech at a Reception at Boston," July 9, 1852, in James McIntyre, ed., *The Writings and Speeches of Daniel Webster*, 18 vols. (Boston: Little, Brown, 1903), vol. 13, p. 529. Unless otherwise indicated, all of my references to Webster's speeches and writings are to this edition by kind permission of the publisher.

2. Daniel Webster, "Speech at Marshfield," July 25, 1852, in James McIntyre, ed., *The Writings and Speeches of Daniel Webster*, 18 vols. (Boston: Little, Brown, 1903), vol. 13, p. 539.

3. Daniel Webster, "Speech at a Reception at Boston," July 9, 1852, in James McIntyre, ed., *The Writings and Speeches of Daniel Webster*, 18 vols. (Boston: Little, Brown, 1903), vol. 13, p. 534.

4. William Lloyd Garrison, "Fourth of July Address, 1829," in George M. Fredrickson, ed., *William Lloyd Garrison* (Englewood Cliffs, N. J.: Prentice-hall, 1968), pp. 16–17.

5. Garrison, "No Union with Slaveholders," *The Liberator* (Boston, May 31, 1844), in Fredrickson, p. 53.

6. Wendell Phillips, *A Review of Webster's Speech on Slavery* (Boston, 1850), p. 3.

7. See Paul C. Nagel, *One Nation Indivisible: The Union in American Thought, 1776–1861* (New York: Oxford University Press, 1964).

8. Theodore Parker, *A Discourse Occasioned by the Death of Daniel Webster* (Boston: Benjamin B. Mussey, 1853), p. 93.

9. Abraham Lincoln to Horace Greeley, August 22, 1862, reprinted in Henry Steele Commager, *Documents of American History,* 7th ed. (New York: Appleton-Century-Crofts, 1963), pp. 417–418.

10. Edwin Percy Whipple, "Daniel Webster as a Master of English Style," *American Literature and Other Papers* (Boston: Houghton Mifflin, 1899), p. 87.

11. Maurice Baxter, *One and Inseparable: Daniel Webster and the Union* (Cambridge: Harvard University Press, 1984.)

12. Daniel Webster, "Fourth of July Oration at Concord, New Hampshire," July 4, 1806, in James McIntyre, ed., *The Writings and Speeches of Daniel Webster,* 18 vols. (Boston: Little, Brown, 1903), vol. 15, p. 537.

13. Daniel Webster, "Slavery and the Constitution," May 22, 1851, in James McIntyre, ed., *The Writings and Speeches of Daniel Webster,* 18 vols. (Boston: Little, Brown, 1903), vol. 4, p. 255.

14. Daniel Webster, "Autobiography," in James McIntyre, ed., *The Writings and Speeches of Daniel Webster,* 18 vols. (Boston: Little, Brown, 1903), vol. 17, p. 6.

15. Ibid., p. 8.

16. George Ticknor Curtis, *Life of Daniel Webster,* 2 vols. (New York: D. Appleton, 1870), vol. 1, p. 18.

17. Daniel Webster, "Autobiography," in James McIntyre, ed., *The Writings and Speeches of Daniel Webster,* 18 vols. (Boston: Little, Brown, 1903), vol. 17, p. 9.

18. Ibid., pp. 9–10.

19. Irving Bartlett, *Daniel Webster* (New York: W.W. Norton, 1978), p. 20.

20. Daniel Webster, "Autobiography," in James McIntyre, ed., *The Writings and Speeches of Daniel Webster,* 18 vols. (Boston: Little, Brown, 1903), vol. 17, p. 10.

21. Ibid., p. 11.

22. Claude Fuess, *Daniel Webster,* 2 vols. (Boston: Little, Brown, 1930), vol. 1, p. 44.

23. Leon Burr Richardson, *History of Dartmouth College* 2 vols. (Hanover: Dartmouth College Publications, 1932), vol. 1, p. 250.

24. Herbert Darling Foster, "Webster and Choate in College: Dartmouth under the Curriculum of 1796–1819," *The Dartmouth Alumni Magazine* 19, 6 (April 1927), pp. 509–519 and 7 (May 1927, pp. 605–616), 6 (April 1927), p. 510.

25. Ibid., p. 511.

26. Ibid., p. 513.

27. Fuess, *Daniel Webster,* vol. 1, p. 53.

28. Daniel Webster to Thomas Merril, January 4, 1803, in James McIntyre, ed., *The Writings and Speeches of Daniel Webster,* 18 vols. (Boston: Little, Brown, 1903), vol. 17, p. 129.

29. Daniel Webster, "Jeremiah Mason," October 14, 1848, in James McIntyre, ed., *The Writings and Speeches of Daniel Webster,* 18 vols. (Boston: Little, Brown, 1903), vol. 4, p. 179.

30. George Ticknor Curtis, *Life of Daniel Webster,* 2 vols. (New York: D. Appleton, 1870), vol. 1, p. 90.

31. See David H. Fischer, *The Revolution in American Conservatism: The Federalist Party in the Era of Jeffersonian Democracy* (New York: Harper, 1965).

32. Daniel Webster, "An Appeal to the Old Whigs of New Hampshire," February, 1805, in James McIntyre, ed., *The Writings and Speeches of Daniel Webster,* 18 vols. (Boston: Little, Brown, 1903), vol. 15, p. 527.

33. Maurice Baxter, *One and Inseparable: Daniel Webster and the Union* (Cambridge: Harvard University Press, 1984), p. 33, citing *Oracle,* July 12, 1812.

34. George Ticknor, *Life and Letters of George Ticknor,* 2 vols. (Boston: James R. Osgood, 1876), vol. 1, p. 330.

35. Daniel Webster, "First Settlement of New England," December 22, 1820, in James McIntyre, ed., *The Writings and Speeches of Daniel Webster,* 18 vols. (Boston: Little, Brown, 1903), vol. 1, p. 255.

36. Curtis, *Life of Daniel Webster,* vol. 1, p. 198.

37. Daniel Webster, "The Revolution in Greece," January 19, 1824, in James McIntyre, ed., *The Writings and Speeches of Daniel Webster,* 18 vols. (Boston: Little, Brown, 1903), vol. 5, p. 65.

38. Curtis, *Life of Daniel Webster,* vol. 1, p. 351.

39. Baxter, *One and Inseparable,* p. 188.

40. Curtis, *Life of Daniel Webster,* vol. 1, p. 386.

41. See Daniel Walker Howe, *The Political Culture of the American Whigs* (Chicago: University of Chicago Press, 1979); also see Thomas Brown, *Politics and Statesmanship* (New York: Columbia University Press, 1985).

42. Daniel Webster, "The Currency," June 1837, in James McIntyre, ed., *The Writings and Speeches of Daniel Webster,* 18 vols. (Boston: Little, Brown, 1903), vol. 13, p. 81.

43. Curtis, *Life of Daniel Webster,* vol. 2. p. 21.

44. Daniel Webster, "The Sub-Treasury and the Organization of the Militia," also known as "Speech at Patchogue," September 22, 1840, in James McIntyre, ed., *The Writings and Speeches of Daniel Webster,* 18 vols. (Boston: Little, Brown, 1903), vol. 13, p. 114.

45. Curtis, *Life of Daniel Webster,* vol. 2, p. 81.

46. Ibid., p. 131.

47. Daniel Webster, "Reception at Boston," September 30, 1842, in James McIntyre, ed., *The Writings and Speeches of Daniel Webster,* 18 vols. (Boston: Little, Brown, 1903), vol. 3. p. 126.

48. Daniel Webster, "Whig Principles," July 4, 1844, in James McIntyre, ed., *The Writings and Speeches of Daniel Webster,* 18 vols. (Boston: Little, Brown, 1903), vol. 13, p. 238.

49. Curtis, *Life of Daniel Webster,* vol. 2, p. 282.

50. Daniel Webster, "The Mexican War," September 29, 1847, in James McIntyre, ed., *The Writings and Speeches of Daniel Webster,* 18 vols. (Boston: Little, Brown, 1903), vol. 13, p. 345.

51. Daniel Webster, "The Free Soil Party," October 9, 1848, in James McIntyre, ed., *The Writings and Speeches of Daniel Webster,* 18 vols. (Boston: Little, Brown, 1903), vol. 13, p. 367.

52. Daniel Webster to Peter Harvey, February 22, 1850, cited in Curtis, *Life,* vol. 2, p. 400.

53. Daniel Webster, "The Constitution and the Union," March 7, 1850, in James McIntyre, ed., *The Writings and Speeches of Daniel Webster,* 18 vols. (Boston: Little, Brown, 1903), vol. 10, pp. 57–58.

54. Daniel Webster to Edward Everett, September 27, 1851, in James McIntyre, ed., *The Writings and Speeches of Daniel Webster,* 18 vols. (Boston: Little, Brown, 1903), vol. 18, p. 473.

55. Theodore Parker, *Speech of Theodore Parker delivered in The Old Cradle of Liberty* (Boston, 1850), p. 35.

56. Wendell Phillips, *A Review of Webster's Speech on Slavery* (Boston, 1850), p. 30.

57. Ralph Waldo Emerson, *The Journals and Miscellaneous Notebooks of Ralph Waldo Emerson,* 16 vols. ed. by Alfred R. Ferguson and Ralph H. Orth (Cambridge: Harvard University Press, 1971) vol. 9, p. 409.

58. Daniel Webster to Peter Harvey, October 2, 1850, in C. H. Van Tyne, *Letters of Daniel Webster* (New York: McClure, Phillips, 1902), p. 433.

59. Curtis, *Life of Daniel Webster,* vol. 2, p. 698.

Chapter Two

1. Herbert Darling Foster, "Webster and Choate in College: Dartmouth under the Curriculum of 1796–1819," *The Dartmouth Alumni Magazine* 19, 6 (April 1927): pp. 509–519 and 7 (May 1927, pp. 605–616); 6 (April 1927), p. 513. See also *Catalogue of the Books in the Library of The United Fraternity at Dartmouth College,* April 1812 (Hanover, NH: Charles Spear, 1812), in the Dartmouth College library. Unfortunately, no catalogue of the fraternity's holdings for the years that Webster spent at Dartmouth exists today.

2. Foster, 6, p. 513.

3. Henry Home, Lord Kames, *The Elements of Criticism,* 2 vols., (Edinburgh: Bell, Creech, Cadell, and Robinson, 1785), vol. 1, p. 88.

4. Ibid., p. 91.

5. Ibid., p. 100.

6. Elihu Smith to E. D. Sanborn, November 10, 1852, in James McIntyre, ed., *The Writings and Speeches of Daniel Webster,* 18 vols. (Boston: Little, Brown, 1903), vol. 17, p. 46.

7. Aaron Loveland, "Reminiscences of Aaron Loveland," typed copy of manuscript in Dartmouth Library archives.

8. My thanks to George C. Jepsen for suggesting this fundamental distinction and for explaining it to me.

9. Daniel Webster, "Oration at Hanover," July 4, 1800, in James McIntyre, ed., *The Writings and Speeches of Daniel Webster,* 18 vols. (Boston: Little, Brown, 1903), vol. 15, p. 475.

10. Edwin Percy Whipple, "Daniel Webster as a Master of English Style," *American Literature and Other Papers* (Boston: Houghton Mifflin, 1899), pp. 232–33.

11. Daniel Webster, "The First Settlement of New England," December 22, 1822, in James McIntyre, ed., *The Writings and Speeches of Daniel Webster,* 18 vols. (Boston: Little, Brown, 1903), vol. 1, p. 183.

12. See for example Philip Freneau's "Advice to Authors. By the Late Mr. Robert Slender," Joel Barlow's introduction to *The Vision of Columbus,* and numerous essays by Charles Brockden Brown. For commentary, see Harry Haydon Clark, "Nationalism in American Literature," *University of Toronto Quarterly,* 2, 4 (July 1933), 492–519.

13. Daniel Webster, "The State of Our Literature," Summer 1809, in James McIntyre, ed., *The Writings and Speeches of Daniel Webster,* 18 vols. (Boston: Little, Brown, 1903), vol. 15, p. 575.

14. Daniel Webster, "Address before the Washington Benevolent Society," July 4, 1802, in James McIntyre, ed., *The Writings and Speeches of Daniel Webster,* 18 vols. (Boston: Little, Brown, 1903), vol. 15, p. 583.

15. Daniel Webster, "The Dignity and Importance of Literature," February 23, 1852, in James McIntyre, ed., *The Writings and Speeches of Daniel Webster,* 18 vols. (Boston: Little, Brown, 1903), vol. 13, p. 463.

16. See David Levin, *History as Romantic Art* (Stanford: Stanford University Press, 1959); Michael Kraus, *A History of American History* (New York: Farrar and Rinehart, 1937); William L. Hedges, "The Myth of the Republic and the Theory of American Literature," *Prospects,* 4 (New York: Burt Franklin, 1979); and Daniel Walker Howe, *The Political Culture of American Whigs* (Chicago: University of Chicago Press, 1979).

Chapter Three

1. G. J. Abbot to Edward Everett, April 12, 1854, in C. H. Van Tyne, ed., *The Letters of Daniel Webster* (New York: McClure, Phillips, 1902), pp. 705–708.

2. Daniel Webster, "The First Settlement of New England," December 22, 1822, in James McIntyre, ed., *The Writings and Speeches of Daniel Webster,* 18 vols. (Boston: Little, Brown, 1903), vol. 1, p. 181.

3. Consider, for example, Webster's mention of "the Puritans who landed upon the rock of Plymouth." He used the terms *Pilgrim* and *Puritan* more or less interchangeably and without regard for their different meanings.

4. See Irving Bartlett, *Daniel Webster* (New York: W.W. Norton, 1978), pp. 80–81; Maurice Baxter, *One and Inseparable: Daniel Webster and the Union* (Cambridge: Harvard University Press, 1984), p. 90.

5. Daniel Webster, "The Bunker Hill Monument," June 17, 1825, in James McIntyre, ed., *The Writings and Speeches of Daniel Webster,* 18 vols. (Boston: Little, Brown, 1903), vol. 1, p. 236.

6. Daniel Webster, "The Completion of the Bunker Hill Monument," June 17, 1843, in James McIntyre, ed., *The Writings and Speeches of Daniel Webster,* 18 vols. (Boston: Little, Brown, 1903), vol. 1, p. 270.

7. Daniel Webster, "The Landing at Plymouth," December 22, 1843, in James McIntyre, ed., *The Writings and Speeches of Daniel Webster,* 18 vols. (Boston: Little, Brown, 1903), vol. 1, p. 209.

8. Wendell Phillips, "The Pilgrims," *The Pilgrims in Speeches, Lectures, and Letters* (Boston: James Redpath, 1863), p. 228.

9. Daniel Webster, "Pilgrim Festival at New York," December 22, 1850, in James McIntyre, ed., *The Writings and Speeches of Daniel Webster,* 18 vols. (Boston: Little, Brown, 1903), vol. 4, pp. 217–218.

10. Abbot to Everett, April 12, 1854, pp. 705–708.

11. See William Alfred Bryan, *George Washington in American Literature: 1775–1865* (New York: Columbia University Press).

12. Daniel Webster, "Oration at Hanover," July 4, 1800, in James McIntyre, ed., *The Writings and Speeches of Daniel Webster,* 18 vols. (Boston: Little, Brown, 1903), vol. 15, p. 481.

13. John Adams to Thomas Jefferson, September 3, 1816, in Lester J. Capon, ed., *The Adams–Jefferson Letters,* 2 vols. (Chapel Hill: The University of North Carolina Press, 1959), 2, p. 488.

14. Daniel Webster, "Fourth of July Oration," July 4, 1802, in James McIntyre, ed., *The Writings and Speeches of Daniel Webster,* 18 vols. (Boston: Little, Brown, 1903), vol. 15, p. 518.

15. Daniel Webster, "Address before the Washington Benevolent Society," July 4, 1812, in James McIntyre, ed., *The Writings and Speeches of Daniel Webster,* 18 vols. (Boston: Little, Brown, 1903), vol. 15, p. 484.

16. Daniel Webster, "The Character of Washington," February 22, 1832, in James McIntyre, ed., *The Writings and Speeches of Daniel Webster,* 18 vols. (Boston: Little, Brown, 1903), vol. 2, pp. 69–70.

17. Daniel Webster, "Speech at Annapolis," March 25, 1851, in James McIntyre, ed., *The Writings and Speeches of Daniel Webster,* 18 vols. (Boston: Little, Brown, 1903), vol. 13, p. 392.

18. Daniel Webster, "The Addition to the Capitol," July 4, 1851, in James McIntyre, ed., *The Writings and Speeches of Daniel Webster,* 18 vols. (Boston: Little, Brown, 1903), vol. 13, p. 316.

19. Daniel Webster, "The Completion of the Bunker Hill Monument," June 17, 1843, vol. 1, p. 281.

Chapter Four

1. Paul C. Nagel, *One Nation Indivisible: The Union in American Thought, 1776–1861* (New York: Oxford University Press, 1964).

2. Daniel Webster to James Hervey Bingham, February 5, 1800, in James McIntyre, ed., *The Writings and Speeches of Daniel Webster,* 18 vols. (Boston: Little, Brown, 1903), vol. 17, p. 78.

3. Daniel Webster, "Oration at Hanover," July 4, 1800, in James McIntyre, ed., *The Writings and Speeches of Daniel Webster,* 18 vols. (Boston: Little, Brown, 1903), vol. 15, pp. 483–484.

4. Daniel Webster, "Fourth of July Oration," July 4, 1802, in James McIntyre, ed., *The Writings and Speeches of Daniel Webster,* 18 vols. (Boston: Little, Brown, 1903), vol. 15, p. 509.

5. George Ticknor Curtis, *Life of Daniel Webster,* 2 vols. (New York: D. Appleton, 1870), vol. 1, p. 95.

6. Daniel Webster, "Considerations on the Embargo," 1808, in James McIntyre, ed., *The Writings and Speeches of Daniel Webster,* 18 vols. (Boston: Little, Brown, 1903), vol. 15, p. 564.

7. Daniel Webster, "Address before the Washington Benevolent Society," July 4, 1812, in James McIntyre, ed., *The Writings and Speeches of Daniel Webster,* 18 vols. (Boston: Little, Brown, 1903), vol. 15, p. 584.

8. Daniel Webster, "The Rockingham Memorial," August 1812, in James McIntyre, ed., *The Writings and Speeches of Daniel Webster,* 18 vols. (Boston: Little, Brown, 1903), vol. 15, p. 600.

9. In 1802 and 1806, Webster concluded pro-Union speeches by calling out for "true patriots" who would unite the country and save America for its destiny by sacrificing their lives if need be to prevent invasion from overseas. "Above fear, above danger, above reproach," he said of

the True Patriot in 1806, "he feels that the last end, which can happen to any man, never comes too soon, if he fall in defense of the law and liberty of his country" (vol. 15, p. 547). Webster used the same image of martyrdom in 1812—with the great difference that this time he meant that the Patriot would resist the "French Faction" as well as the French:

[If] it be in the righteous counsel of Heaven to bury New England, her religion, her government, and her laws, under the throne of foreign despotism, there are those among her sons, that will never live to see that event. . . . They cannot perish better than standing between their country and the embraces of a ferocious tyranny, hated of man, accursed of God. At the appointed time, they will embrace that martyrdom, not only with fortitude, but with cheerfulness; resolved, in all events, that when they shall for the last time behold the light of that sun, or look on the pleasant verdure of those fields, it shall not be with the eyes of slaves and subjects of impious despotism. (vol. 15, pp. 597–598)

On the surface, Webster was talking about fighting the French, but the issue of the day was not resistance to France. It was disagreement with a Federal policy that threatened New England's local interests. To a person with this on his or her mind, "foreign despotism" could very well mean the distant government in Washington.

10. Maurice G. Baxter, *Daniel Webster and the Supreme Court;* also Baxter, *One and Inseparable,* especially chapter 10, "Lawyer."

11. Daniel Webster, *McCulloch* v. *Maryland,* in James McIntyre, ed., *The Writings and Speeches of Daniel Webster,* 18 vols. (Boston: Little, Brown, 1903), vol. 15, p. 365.

12. George Ticknor Curtis, *Life of Daniel Webster,* 2 vols. (New York: D. Appleton, 1870), vol. 1, p. 531.

13. Daniel Webster, "Second Speech on Foot's Resolution," also known as "The Second Reply to Hayne," January 26 and 27, 1830, in James McIntyre, ed., *The Writings and Speeches of Daniel Webster,* 18 vols. (Boston: Little, Brown, 1903), vol. 6, p. 3.

14. Robert Y. Hayne, *Speech on Mr. Foot's Resolution* (Philadelphia: T. B. Peterson, 1830), p. 23.

15. Daniel Webster, "Second Speech on Foot's Resolution," January 26 and 27, 1830, vol. 6, p. 14.

16. The custom of addressing the Senate is to direct speeches to the presiding officer. That is usually a meaningless device, but since Vice President John C. Calhoun was the officer in question, the formality was pointed that day.

17. Daniel Webster, "Second Speech on Foot's Resolution," January 26 and 27, 1830, vol. 6, p. 54.

18. Edmund Burke, *A Philosophical Inquiry into the Origins of Our Ideas of the Sublime and the Beautiful,* in Louis I. Bredvold, Alan D.

McKillop, Lois Whitney, and John M. Bullitt, *Eighteenth-Century Poetry and Prose,* 3rd ed. (New York: The Ronald Press, 1973), p. 1104.

19. Daniel Webster, "Dangers to the Constitution," also known as, "Presentation of a Vase," October 12, 1835, in James McIntyre, ed., *The Writings and Speeches of Daniel Webster,* 18 vols. (Boston: Little, Brown, 1903), vol. 2, pp. 177, 179.

20. Daniel Webster, "Views on Public Questions," also known as "Speech at Niblo's Saloon," March 15, 1837, in James McIntyre, ed., *The Writings and Speeches of Daniel Webster,* 18 vols. (Boston: Little, Brown, 1903), vol. 2, p. 199.

21. Daniel Webster, "Congressional Power under the Constitution," also known as "Speech at Albany," August 27, 1844, in James McIntyre, ed., *The Writings and Speeches of Daniel Webster,* 18 vols. (Boston: Little, Brown, 1903), vol. 3, p. 227.

22. Daniel Webster, "The State of Georgia," also known as "Speech at Savannah, Georgia," May 26, 1847, in James McIntyre, ed., *The Writings and Speeches of Daniel Webster,* 18 vols. (Boston: Little, Brown, 1903), vol. 4, p. 96.

23. Daniel Webster, "The Constitution and The Union," March 7, 1850, in James McIntyre, ed., *The Writings and Speeches of Daniel Webster,* 18 vols. (Boston: Little, Brown, 1903), vol. 10, p. 62.

24. Daniel Webster, "The Addition to the Capitol," July 4, 1851, in James McIntyre, ed., *The Writings and Speeches of Daniel Webster,* 18 vols. (Boston: Little, Brown, 1903), vol. 4, p. 293.

Chapter Five

1. Abraham Lincoln to Horace Greeley, August 22, 1862, reprinted in Henry Steele Commager, *Documents of American History,* 7th ed. (New York: Appleton-Century-Crofts, 1963), pp. 417–418.

2. Daniel Webster, "Second Speech on Foot's Resolution," also known as "The Second Reply to Hayne," January 26 and 27, 1830, in James McIntyre, ed., *The Writings and Speeches of Daniel Webster,* 18 vols. (Boston: Little, Brown, 1903), vol. 6, p. 70.

3. Daniel Webster, "The Character of Washington," February 22, 1832, in James McIntyre, ed., *The Writings and Speeches of Daniel Webster,* 18 vols. (Boston: Little, Brown, 1903), vol. 2, p. 81.

4. Daniel Webster, "Views on Public Questions," also known as "Speech at Niblo's Saloon," March 15, 1837, in James McIntyre, ed., *The Writings and Speeches of Daniel Webster,* 18 vols. (Boston: Little, Brown, 1903), vol. 2, p. 199.

5. Daniel Webster, "Oration at Hanover," July 4, 1800, in James McIntyre, ed., *The Writings and Speeches of Daniel Webster,* 18 vols. (Boston: Little, Brown, 1903), vol. 15, p. 479.

6. Daniel Webster, "The Bunker Hill Monument," June 17, 1825, in James McIntyre, ed., *The Writings and Speeches of Daniel Webster,* 18 vols. (Boston: Little, Brown, 1903), vol. 1, p. 237.

7. Daniel Webster, "The Completion of the Bunker Hill Monument," June 17, 1843, in James McIntyre, ed., *The Writings and Speeches of Daniel Webster,* 18 vols. (Boston: Little, Brown, 1903), vol. 1, p. 265.

8. Daniel Webster, "Speech at Concord, New Hampshire," also known as "The Jackson Administration," October, 1834, in James McIntyre, ed., *The Writings and Speeches of Daniel Webster,* 18 vols. (Boston: Little, Brown, 1903), vol. 13, p. 55.

9. Daniel Webster, "Speech at Capon Springs, Virginia," also known as "The Union of the States," June 28, 1851, in James McIntyre, ed., *The Writings and Speeches of Daniel Webster,* 18 vols. (Boston: Little, Brown, 1903), vol. 13, p. 434.

10. Daniel Webster, "Remarks at a Public Reception at Bangor, Maine," also known as "The Limitations and Restraints of the Constitution," August 25, 1835, in James McIntyre, ed., *The Writings and Speeches of Daniel Webster,* 18 vols. (Boston: Little, Brown, 1903), vol. 2, p. 165.

11. Daniel Webster, "The Constitution and the Union," March 7, 1850, in James McIntyre, ed., *The Writings and Speeches of Daniel Webster,* 18 vols. (Boston: Little, Brown, 1903), vol. 10, pp. 57–58.

12. Daniel Webster, "The Dignity and Importance of History," February 23, 1852, in James McIntyre, ed., *The Writings and Speeches of Daniel Webster,* 18 vols. (Boston: Little, Brown, 1903), vol. 13, p. 495.

13. Webster quoted Revelations 18:2 in Greek. I have substituted for his words the King James translation.

14. Daniel Webster, "The Currency," also known as "Speech at St. Louis," June, 1837, in James McIntyre, ed., *The Writings and Speeches of Daniel Webster,* 18 vols. (Boston: Little, Brown, 1903), vol. 13, p. 80.

15. Daniel Webster, "The Revolution in Greece," January 19, 1824, in James McIntyre, ed., *The Writings and Speeches of Daniel Webster,* 18 vols. (Boston: Little, Brown, 1903), vol. 5, pp. 62–63.

16. Daniel Webster, "New Hampshire and Her Sons," also known as "Festival of the Sons of New Hampshire," November 7, 1849, in James McIntyre, ed., *The Writings and Speeches of Daniel Webster,* 18 vols. (Boston: Little, Brown, 1903), vol. 4, p. 197.

17. Daniel Webster, "The First Settlement of New England," December 22, 1820, in James McIntyre, ed., *The Writings and Speeches of Daniel Webster,* 18 vols. (Boston: Little, Brown, 1903), vol. 1, p. 182.

18. Daniel Webster, "The Increase of Executive Power," also known as "Speech at the Whig Convention," October 5, 1840, in James McIntyre, ed., *The Writings and Speeches of Daniel Webster,* 18 vols. (Boston: Little, Brown, 1903), vol. 3, p. 102.

19. Ernst Cassirer, "The Technique of Our Modern Political Myths," *Symbol, Myth and Culture* (New Haven: Yale University Press, 1979), pp. 240–270; p. 246.

20. Daniel Webster, "Adams and Jefferson," August 2, 1826, in James McIntyre, ed., *The Writings and Speeches of Daniel Webster,* 18 vols. (Boston: Little, Brown, 1903), vol. 1, p. 307–308.

Index

(1841), 29; negotiates Treaty of
Washington, 30–31; breaks with
Lowell, 31; leaves Tyler
administration, 32; campaigns
for Clay (1844), 32–33; attacked
by Ingersoll and Yancey, 34–35;
deaths of two children, 35;
tours southern states (1847), 35;
defeated in nomination bid
(1848), 36; supports
Compromise of 1850, 37–40;
85 ff.; becomes Secretary of
State (1850), 39; believes Union
safe, 39; involvement in
Kossuth Affair, 40; defeated in
1852 Whig convention, 1, 40;
death, 40; on the study of law,
16; on poetry, 49, 51; on
artistic genius, 51; on history,
55 ff.; on "truthfulness", 55–56;
on Pilgrims, 63–78; on George
Washington, 48, 78–88, 116

Speeches and writings (listed
alphabetically):
"Adams and Jefferson" (Boston,
Massachusetts; August 2, 1826),
23, 128–29

"Addition to the Capitol"
(Washington, D.C.; July 4,
1851), 86–87, 108–112

"Albany" a.k.a. "Congressional
Power under the Constitution"
(Albany, New York; August 27,
1844), 106

"Annapolis" (Annapolis,
Maryland; March 25, 1851),
85–86

"Appeal to the Old Whigs of
New Hampshire" (1805), 17, 18

"Bangor, Maine" a.k.a. "The
Limitations and Restraints of
the Constitution" (Bangor,
Maine; August 23, 1835), 120

"Bunker Hill Monument"
(Charleston, Massachusetts;
June 17, 1825), 23, 69–70,
87–88, 117–118, 124–125

"Capon Springs" (Capon Springs,
Virginia; June 28, 1858), 119

"Character of Washington"
(Washington, D.C.; February 22,
1832), 82–85, 115

"Completion of the Bunker Hill
Monument" (Charleston,
Massachusetts; June 17, 1843),
71–72, 118–119

"Concord, New Hampshire" a.k.a.
"The Jackson Administration"
(Concord, New Hampshire;
October, 1834), 119

"Considerations on the Embargo"
(1808), 17, 94–95

"Constitution and Union" a.k.a.
"Seventh of March" (U.S.
Senate; March 7, 1850), 37–38,
107–108, 120–121

"Constitution not a Compact
Between the States" (U.S.
Senate; February 16, 1833), 106

"Currency" (St. Louis, Missouri;
June, 1837), 27, 122–123